Phoenix Papers

26 Lawrence Poets

ISBN: 0-9632475-1-4 Library of Congress Catalog Number: 93-083842
PENTHE Publishing Co., P.O. Box 994 Lawrence, KS 66044
Printed in the United States of America

Phoenix Papers
26 Lawrence Poets

Edited by **Stephen Addiss and Stanley Lombardo**

Designed by **Lois Greene**

Cover photography by **Terry Evans**

An **Enso** Book

A special imprint of PENTHE Publishing Company
Lawrence, KS

Contents

Introduction

I think of my grandmother in Newton, Kansas, during the 1920's, reading Tu Fu and Li Po between women's club meetings and choir practice. She knew the British canon of poetry from school, and Longfellow and James Whitcomb Riley—in those days grade school children memorized rhymes starting with kindergarten. But in that small town, remote on the flat croplands, the T'ang Dynasty poets spoke to her most intimately. Lawrence, Kansas, in the 1990's is not remote in the same way as my grandmother's town and time, but when Steve Addiss and Stanley Lombardo decided to collect this anthology of Lawrence poets, they found a striking number of Asian-influenced works. This is but one of many surprises in this collection.

Lawrence is an uncommon place, its population skewed by the presence of the state's major research university. This selection of poets centers around the university—only Trish Reeves, an instructor at Haskell Indian Junior College, has never taught or been a student at the University of Kansas. Despite the academic influence, the work is mostly not formalist (an exception being Judith Roitman's pantoums). Certainly the landscape appears in these pieces, and the extremities of weather. Many of the writers are native Kansans, and the rest are touched by years in this place at the edge of the Kaw (or Kansas) River, at the edge between grassland and forest, the edge of the Ice Age glaciation. Transition marks the landscape: rocks are a mixture of Pennsylvanian limestone (two million years old) and quartzite glacial erratics; plant species include wetlands trillium and high plains bluestem; eagles nest in local reservoirs while prairielands quail hide alongside city roads. Suburbs of Lawrence reach to Topeka on the west and Kansas City on the east, yet oppossums, beavers, muskrats, badgers, deer and foxes are common.

Within this melange of influences, surrealism is often a mode: perhaps this is unexpected in a collection of midwestern poets, but it is no more irrational than the reality Steven Bunch writes about in "Dog Days": a graduate student once kept Einstein's brain in Wichita. The northern lights sometimes appear at this latitude, or sometimes night lights are only the illusion of "fog over the airport lights" (Caryn Mirriam-Goldberg, "About Desire"). In this country tornados can wad up cars and leave them in tree limbs.

Chinese and Buddhist images do not seem out of place in the river/city/prairie borderlands. Roy Gridley's selection of poems is based on a trip to China, and George Wedge writes of a doomed marriage in "Two Roads to Cho-Fu-Sa." Jim Bogan reworks Confucian precepts to fit contemporary times in "Virtuous Amusements and Wicked Demons." References to Bhodisattvas and Buddha appear several places, and Tibetan deities—"Lords of the Soil"—are active in Ken Irby's prose poem set in southeastern Kansas.

Perhaps less often represented are narratives about people. Fragments of stories are present, like the funeral scene of "Photos: November" (by Anne Wallace) and George Allen's dogs chasing coyotes in "Address Unknown" (by Jim McCrary) or the abuse of a girl in "Inanna: Seven Gates" (by Jane Hoskinson), but the shading is ultimately lyric, about reflection or the language process of the narrator. Few of these poets work in the form of long narrative poems.

Many of the *Phoenix Papers* writers have published books, including Victor Contoski, Ken Irby, Michael L. Johnson, Philip Kimball, Jim McCrary, John Moritz, and Trish Reeves. All have previous publications in journals; these range from *Exquisite Corpse* to *Avec* to *Conjunctions* to *Kansas Quarterly*. Many of these writers have been published at one time or another in *Cottonwood*, associated with the KU English department, or (and) by Tansy Press, edited by John Moritz since the late 1960's. All continue to be active writers, and though there are friendships among many of these individuals, no distinct "school" of writing predominates. Included in these pages are examples of free verse, surrealism, language poetry, prose poems, found poems, and patterned poems. References to the works of Charles Olson and Andre Breton and Walt Whitman appear, but in individualized ways.

This is not a collection of poems about Lawrence or about Kansas though some localities do appear, like the Flamingo Club, site of the Poetry Slams ("Lunch at the Flamingo Club" by Michael L. Johnson), and the sweep of highway from Colorado to Lawrence ("Precambrian Slab" by John Moritz). This is a collection of writings about possibilities of the mind, whether inspired by winter winds or the poetry of Chinese masters.

Denise Low

Ken Irby

I have fetched phoenix papers

[After a a gift of poems from Roy Gridley, written while travelling in China, left silently at the door between 11 am and noon, 28 Jul
1986]

The referential is the clear telling. What is remembered or not remembered of the dream is of another life. Memory itself is from another life. Cups, called so simply, are not sufficient to account for their overflow. The things that you want to be quick, the things that you want to be more specific, do not account for the power of their sentimentality, for the cough, for their touching their shadows. A loss, then, if we do not, but *never doubt that the world of men can share this knowledge.*

•

There we have gone off along the railroad tracks into, to school, and stop and dip our feet in the creek, just for a little while, to cool and cool, with our little brothers and sisters. That is the distance, and in that it does not return, memory itself is from so long ago, no matter how long ago it instantly is of. And the try to intensify wreaks the comparison, to keep compassionate.

The epigraph and the quotation in the first paragraph are from A.C. Graham's translation of Li Shang-yin's "The Walls of Emerald", in *Poems of the Late T'ang* (Penguin. 1965).

Ken Irby

late in the Winter when thaws beginning Spring should long ago have started, the cold persists, no more heavy snows but frozen mists, thin sleets, leftover snow grimy, brooding the woods, the yards, the trash in upper rooms waiting for brighter, warmer days to be taken out, bent over above the porches, waiting, for footsteps soon to come, and talk, up there

I used to go up in the late afternoons, not long before sunset, and sit in the bare attic, looking out West and North, toward the river, the hills on the other side of the flood plain brighter than anything else in the day, snowdark the woods—and watch till the aftersunset glow had vanished and the room was dark, the earth turn

the space of time in a life between a year of waking and a year of sleeping, to wake again, and then go downstairs, turn on the lamps in the living room, put on some music out of the shadows, make a drink, start fixing dinner—and the life too would come into the room, out of the burrow of earth under the snow in the woods, like the figure of a dog molded in snow in the woods, shake, and rouse itself, and come in

Ken Irby

I met the Angel Sus on the Skin Bridge
the Bridge Chinvat, offertory
my image crossing the basketball court and taking the path into the woods
and at the other end, in the gravel at the bend of Terrace Road
more expressive than the small red heart-shaped lips of the Lizard Mother, your endlessly mobile face
snout cloud of light and bristles thicket of impenetrable brightness
and smile of infinite frenzied utter patience
nostrils as close to my brow as opened clover
only a face! only a face! only a face!
wings but the knot clod sfumato uncertain noose clothing
over the skin we share, organ me you share
was it John telling me to turn to you, in crowded Houlihan's on the Plaza, with Charlie and the bears in the dark
brought me to you, you came out this far to meet me
where the VW's been parked since at least last March and the horses' empty field comes in close and the houses begin
"You must make me the Clean Compound
first, before you pass through me"
each to each?

Ken Irby

a silence in the Central Tree
the leaves gone down the autumn flood and winter frozen
barest branch click
only occasionally

who left the prints?   hearing us?   we missed?

sap listeners   tree leavers   bark gnawers   wind freaks

from-the-sky-who-dwells-*in*-the-tree?   "foolish to think"

«earth-bedded servants of the unsilent bowl»   "people live there"

«and with unwashen feet»

birdless, empty   and yet the great space all
«packed full of ominous sound»

still
can you hear it
tell?

Ken Irby

[for Jonathan Williams' 50th birthday]

According to the *Vita Metrica* of his life, Pindar died in Argos at the age of 80 (probably in 438 BC). In the words of the Suda lexicon:

> His life ended as he had wished it to; in answer to his prayer for the finest of life's blessings, he met death quickly in the theater, lying in the arms of his beloved Theoxenus.
>
> [tr. Roy Arthur Swanson, *Pindar's Odes* (Bobbs-Merrill, 1974)]

Theoxenus came from an illustrious family of the island of Tenedos (present-day Bozcaada), South of the entrance to the Dardanelles. For his brother, Aristagoras, on his election to the ruling council or Prytaneia of the island, Pindar wrote his *Nemean* 11, and for Theoxenus this passionate encomium and declaration of love, one of his last poems (fragment 108 Bowra, 123 Snell, 131 Turyn). This version, it can't be called a translation, this paraphrase of Pindar's great condensed ode is offered with every debt acknowledged to the renderings in Swanson, in Bowra's *Pindar* (Oxford, 1964), and in Constantine Trypanis' *Penguin Book of Greek Verse* (1971)—to a poet for whom, in Whitman's words, «Bodies are all spiritual.—All words are spiritual—nothing is more spiritual than words».

My heart, we ought to pick the buds of love
when they fit our years
but whoever just catches sight of the flashes
burning out of the eyes of Theoxenus
not carried off in the breakers of desire
had his black heart hammered out of bronze and iron

in an ice fire
Unexalted by Dark-eyed Aphrodite
he drudges desperately for gold
or shameless as a hooker
flutters every street, propositioning the soul
But because of Her I am eaten by that heat

and melt like the wax of divine bees
every time I look at the fresh-fleshed youth of boys
Surely by Puget also
Seduction dwells, and Favor
has brought up the son of Edgar

Ken Irby

The place of the Lord of Soil is down close to the ground—but in the Himalayas he looms from a ridge pole on the road out of town, small silver lead skull bursting into a golden trident of flames, out of a black fur barrel chest, immense.

There is over all of it, for all the landscape not visible, a melody of lost pastoral, of another land altogether of this same place to which the worship has come. Lord of Division.

Here it is a hillside crossing, of the way up from under catalpa trees and the back dirt streets, dusty, to the downtown, West, and the persistent line of the small town mysteries of the prairies, dividing into brick and concrete, paved and dirt, tall grass and short, crow and cardinal, even the Lodge once into North and South.

But now only the sunset dregs and tree tops are visible West, and around us the lights of the Othick Park softball field are on, and the Southeast Kansas semipro Lords of the Soil are warming up, the pitchers we'd come to see most of all. And we stared into the darkness beyond the outfield, across Buck Run and the Frisco tracks, and into the call home from playing late, a vista lower down and more Southerly, of the first pale military perchers on the bluff over the Marmaton, watching the Leavenworth-Gibson road come cattycorner out of the Indians, who were Lords of the Land but not of the Soil, and make the grand division North and South for this piddly corner of the Osages' screwed out of free lands. If the ball flew on out of the arc of the pitcher's intended slash but still with the pitcher's magic from behind his back and in the great wheel of the saluting arm, it would go on wild light and forever, Southwest till it struck the last setting sun of winter solstice on the last barren Cortezed stretch of the Bay of Baja California, and explode like a puffball the way straight into the land of the under world, which is what the Lord of Soil guards, opens, and grins at, for we fear to enter there.

Ken Irby

At dawn, visitors from the farthest stars enter the open door from the balcony, silently, stand, muse, stare down at the sleepers, and weave about the bed entwining figures in the air with spruce boughs, in one hand, and in the other, rattles, making no sound, only stirring the air, rattling the walnut's leaves beyond the door. Slowly one foot is lifted and brought down heavily, then the other, the thunder from the stars to earth heard only in the dreamers' caverns. Footsteps and restlessness. In the slow confusion of waking up, the visitors fade from the room. The vestige of a memory of some great presence returns suddenly, fleetingly, later, during the day, the next, or another, the unintended, primordial, ever-recurring presence of Disturbance

Ed Brunt

The Brunts
2112 North 27th Avenue
Omaha, Nebraska 68111

It is no longer there; a highway came through years ago,
Uprooting its life, scattering its people, changing its name
To something dismal—the North Freeway they called it.
They said it spoke of progress.
I saw no progress.
Sometimes I pass by there and see the ghosts...shadows
And shades of little brown boys and girls who bore
The strangest names: "Ol' Black Ray," "Sonny," "Scooter,"
"Briney," "Beaver," "Rabbit," "Fat Lee," "Kim-the-Boxhead."
They never knew that despite their childish plans, lives
And unions do not remain conveniently intact.

68111

I remember people saying that even the zip code spoke of poverty.
"Oh, you live in that area." Shame never came while
Living there. Shame only came upon venturing outside—
Safety in the company of your own, you know.

The Marble Man

There are many whose faces I can't recall, merely the feelings
Of good or bad...the grizzled landlord, "Old Lady Roach"
Who never let her ward out to play with us "hoodlum niggas,"
The marble man—ah, yes—he was the most famous. They said
He liked little boys. Stories were told—stories of what
He would do to you if he caught you out at night alone.
During the day he collected marbles. But at night only
Hushed whispers, the fear of legend.
Children will be children. Still, no one ventured very far
Into the darkness.

Alleys

Concrete covers what once were alleys, alleys behind houses
        Not fit for human habitation, alleys which gave credence
To spontaneous generation—life from carnage—alleys which
        Served as battlegrounds, clubhouses, escape routes; alleys
In which manhood was explored and sexualities discovered—
        Dirty, filthy, rut-ridden, vegetation-hidden alleys.
Schools never taught these basics.

Moving Day

It came like a lumbering juggernaut, moving some deeper
        Into the darkness, causing others to assimilate themselves
Into "lighter" areas...manicured lawns, clean streets...
        Seeking an acceptance which has yet to come. "There
Goes the neighborhood." Only memories remain, memories of a time
        Of ignorance. Perhaps it really is bliss. No one told them
There was a better side to life. No one told them
        The price.

Darkened Spectre

It is no longer there; a highway came through years ago,
        Uprooting its life, scattering its people, changing its name
To something dismal—the North Freeway they called it.
        They said it spoke of progress, but to change the landscape
Does not change the people. The people have not changed.
        There has been no progress.
Now the thousands of people pass by, eagerly pursuing their
        People lives, their people dreams.
They do not see,
        As I see, the shadows.
They do not know,
        As I know, that histories cannot be retrieved—

        The cold concrete and unyielding pillars, the darkened
Spectre of lives once intertwined.

John Moritz

Precambrian Slab

unravel travail & you get Bolero spewing out a mobius ribbon
from the tapedeck
on the high plains of a slow confluence when yesterday was the heart
of a subterranean turbine on the *industrial walk*
now even lunch is difficult off the afternoon roll Junction City
makes of Seoul food, asian whores & shopkeepers who have followed
the tents to Ft. Riley
& tolerance is a Brinkley goat gland transplant to *keep it up &* swinging
across the radio foam promise to have the whole world *in your hands*
with Reichian joy
going east means make it quick & uneventful
after coming down from the foothills last night drinking coffee & cognac
with chocolates served on a silver tray
back to the mosaic of cheeseburger, home & beer, *the elms are dying*
on the way irrigation circles are jerking corn west of Salina
where the testament is in full form, *go for the loot!* as big as the bottom
line on a billboard
while BBQ Bob plays the washboard blues from a Boulder rooftop

what this country really needs is another ice age

John Moritz

Postcard

for Idaho

re Ann Waldman's reading
she made us eat the headlines
of greed & dysfunction
with the voice of a noisy neighbor

Postcard

for Moscow

Cunt strummed cicada nights in the back yard
where once a yucca bloomed now only an echo

Big mamma whore you were all Babylon for me
those years before

the last invasion of Christ

John Moritz

Poem for Halloween

includes chairs
hanging
            hanging from the ceiling
Crowley on the deck
            with bitter kisses
to stir the world for a moment

six Busoni sonatinas in the groove
we drink coffee & cognac
after Busoni, Cole Porter, the legionaire
of cocaine,
            ...all my stars are random delights
on this Walpurgis night

so my scorpion keeps her tongue
in my ear
            for the torque

John Moritz

"In fact the debasement of
coin really begins when the
design ceased to be cared for."
Ezra Pound

"As long as there are nickels
there'll be buffalo."
Roy Gridley

the sun goes down while heaven waits
& Sappho's moon shines brighter than a flashy coin

Devonne's enigmatic smile could redeem this world
like a flood, if stars were nickels to our thoughts

O Roy, if stars were nickels to our thoughts
she'd drop them in her pocket

Tony Allard

I Am An Ambulance

I am an ambulance and I need lots of fresh corpses to
make my rear-view mirrors move liquid through the night.
The faster I drive the faster the horizon line in my rear-
view mirrors slips off the knife tip and dies. I am a
father ambulance and I need lots of fresh corpses to keep my
desires between the ditches. I am a mother ambulance and I
need lots of dead clock faces to make my mirrors move
through the black night. I am a screaming fist ambulance
and I do so badly need blue-hot speed to make it through
this wide, black night.

Tony Allard

Song Light

Sometimes the moon is a lip that tightens at the thought of making love until it is all over. Some things never change. Just the sight of barely parted lips can bring down a mind, make rubble of the course of planetary logic, unmake the minds of gods. I favor the twisted view: a burning piano, savage hands of the clock slicing open nerve junctures, and one thousand and one bloody sheep crossing a dark, winding road. And if this is not love enough, there is always the seventh vertebra on which to stand and view the whistling glacial chill we all sooner or later begin to sing with.

Tony Allard

Jesus Getting Spanked by the Virgin Mary

The baby Jesus is sprawled across the purring lap of the Virgin Mary. Everything feels like fur and soft eyes and smooth love. Then, in a twentieth century panic, the Virgin Mary begins spanking little Jesus's moon butt. Well, you know there is gonna be a fight for his scorched soul, and sure enough, Mary Magdalene comes storming in, staggering under the weight of her long, blondish hair. She bends down and begins mopping her golden locks on the feet of the Virgin Mary. The Virgin Mary, thinking she is now Jesus Christ, sprawls herself across the clanking, rusty lap of the twentieth century, waiting to be reborn, like the halo of Jesus which is now smashed in a million pieces, sparkling in the dust of his freshly spanked soul.

Tony Allard

A True Dictionary of Definitions: Selections

BRAIN: a stormy sea spills over into the logic of paying attention. Of course, attention is three miles wide and two miles high with no depth and a little naked woman singing church hymns in the lower left hand corner.

BRICKS: chimneys are frozen grandmothers, the smoke being a comfortable thought of a healthy, language-infested baby. Up it goes.

CANOE: when the snow melts, pictures of tall buildings in New York are capable of floating on water.

CAR KEYS: the thin ice on the pond we visited last winter is now gone, and it's July. My pockets have dampness in them and a destined rendezvous with moving metal.

DOUBT: so what if god cannot spell. These wet souls were meant to be slept in.

DRAWING: Bodhisattva in the salt shaker with Marcel Duchamp pictures floating in salty water in my head. Thank goodness the sun has come up.

EARTH: knifing through the slag heap at the Chrysler plant, I suddenly thought myself to be an astronaut looking down at a ball bearing as if it resembled a brain cell contained in a glass of orange juice sitting on the table at my mother-in-law's house.

EPISTEMOLOGY: he had one of those really nice high-speed brains. Every time he would go to the market the words "laundry baskets" would leak out of his mouth instead of, "Excuse me. Is my cart in your way?"

GLOVES: ten minutes into a long sickness I go outside and an old Styrofoam cup blows by. A wet rock and a cat purring are next.

HEAT: fucking motorcycle, you drank all of my soft adrenalin. Now get me some milk at the store, and I will tell tomorrow that she cannot come out and play.

HOME: Six steps off the cliff a tapping on my heart tells me that god is a broken drumhead, and twelve dark nights of the soul equals one trip to the meat market down at the local grocery store.

KISSING: a dictionary props up a broken bedpost. My lover has the most beautiful alphabet clinging to her aura. Don't move. I'll get a net.

LIGHT SWITCH: damn right it is the airplane that defines the Twentieth Century. After all, how else do words get from me to you if it were not for paying the light bill so I can see.

LIVING ROOM CHAIR: unlike space travel, gravity clings to my chair like a wet blanket soaked in ice cream.

LOVE: brought to life by the demands of space between the quotation marks. Each to the other, straight as the crow thinks: this is flight.

LOVERS: the books were so neatly stacked in a pile that she hardly noticed it when his eyes left for the Mexican border.

MELANCHOLIA: a tape recorder is sucking on my wife's breast. I can see little white drops of the Twentieth Century exiting her breast and entering the electromagnetic heart of the little tape recorder heads.

MY LIPS: a true addiction. Geometry lessons never stick to a kiss. After all, saying the name of your lover is a trembling kind of shapeless, nameless memory that skids off the runway and burns up.

RADIO STATION: given the intake manifold on a V-6 engine, the car could easily become a vision of a poem being sucked through a body at the speed of sound.

SHOE LACE: laboring under the illusion of talking cameras, I decide to take a vacation out on the top of my garden rake. Cars emerge from the gumbo of earth, sticky with car lust.

SKY: the stuff the eyelashes row through, creating little wakes of wind, fanning my cheeks. The eyelash breeze makes me think that I don't ever want to call anything a poem, or stop breathing—one of the two.

STRAWBERRY: a tunnel made from old vacation slides is projected on a Russian-like country situated neatly between a blue bottle and one gulp of vodka from a plastic cup.

WATER TOWER: as snow melts, faster than a grapefruit rots, I pull my hand towards the past and lick an old photo of a snowman I built when I was eight years old. I lick a stamp and want to send the photo to the Secretary of Defense so he can lick it too. The checkbook sits next to the grapefruit, rotting much more slowly, and more quietly.

Denise Low

Enantiodromia

Another man drowned in the river,
below the dam, his spirit held
under the rocks until he joined
the others—sand, turtles, and carp.
Sleeping in his boat, too late
he found the current no dream
but more real than his mother
and children. He tumbled calmly
over the dam, braced only for a swim.
Downriver his friend popped loose
when he settled under the river,
quietly, with the minnows.
Light gradually dissolved.

This killer river gives birth each day,
flowing across town in pipes.
People bathe in it, wash clothes,
and water all the dogs,
dumbly alive, and we wonder
at this man plunging into lifeblood
of the city while squirrels chew seeds,
leaves breathe, and a pregnant woman
folds the last of the laundry, sighs,
and drinks deeply from a glass of water.

Denise Low

Starwater

Nursing my first baby
I drank eight glasses of water,
two quarts each day. He grew.

I felt like a carrier for water,
passing it on through to the child,
and some day his child, too,
will fatten, remarkable
like peaches and muskmelons
leaching juice from bare dirt.

Astronomers tell us star dust
once swirled together,
cooled into rocks and water
and still circulates,
the same matter pulled into stars
and Earth and into our flesh.

So water travels the skies,
stretches into clouds,
and falls, moving ever East,
circling, the same ancient water
caught in the whirlwind
binding us all together,
gravity, or maybe, as we know it,
love, or water drawing
together all its kin.

Denise Low

Yellow Woman

The river is a woman of yellow sand.
I lie down in her, leaving a print
of hips and breasts. Soft water touches inside me.

All afternoon I lie under her skin of water and sunheat.
Her brown body dances in all directions.
As we travel, unmoving, closer to dusk, I understand

I would follow a lover down crumbling banks
to warm sand and lie with him,
leaving behind even the children.

I would wash him in riverwater,
our hair smelling of willows. We would fall
asleep and remember the woman,

Yellow Woman, who fashions sand into catfish,
who spreads over a man and tastes
his ears, his teeth and lips, his sweet salt

as sticks float down the current, and cottonwood leaves.
We would forget everything but this river
that carried us into life.

Denise Low

Tulip Elegy–II

Geese bleat over the roof, conversing
somehow with stars as we drowse
beneath constellations of beating wings.
Rearranging staggered lines they steer
a sunward pattern, calling out
as they fly, naming the long way.

Below, under shovels of dirt
the dead move imperceptibly,
turning into other shapes of life.
Tulip bulbs shift under dark horizons
of winter and wedge against years
of decayed shale. Shoots form within,

still trapped, and a miniature blossom
waits in each bleached kernel. Last spring
winged leaves fed this future and wilted.
Now, unmoved by geese or moonlight,
bulbs listen through solstice nightfall
for the searing call of one hot star.

Denise Low

Tulip Elegy–VIII

Resurrection is a falsehood.
The Danish man buried in peat,
stomach filled with spring seeds,
cord around his neck, did not rise
and return to his old mother.
Only barley and rye came to life
as swampwater seeped into his veins.

The *penitente* in New Spain
nailed to a pinewood cross
as cousins guard the highway–
this young man will not revive,
gash himself again with thorns
and offer blood rosaries to Mary.
His last sight will be red dirt,

particles of mountains and woody roots
stewed together with snowmelt.
Dirt is where miracles occur,
where blossoms, kings, and wolves
come part in final union.
Last year's tulip's disassemble
with stripped bones and clay.

New buds this spring are not
the same flowers resurrected.
They are strangers, never before
seen, born just this once.
Petals are fragile butterflies,
brief spans of tissue to measure
only a half-moon life.

Bulbs live on below, secret,
safe but alone, mothers
who sacrifice all their children
while they become hard knots
and endure. Each year they barter
with the dead around them, swell
with new hope and wait.

Roy Gridley

Women and Rain

The august lotus rattle to a roar, rain so heavy Old Hua's sweetcorn leaves but whisper when the three glee-filled young men wade, surge

with nets into the water to seine for leaping carp. Out on the bank three women, all with child, call out, laugh and pat their bellies.

Perched above in a small pavilion two alien voices begin in descant upon the frailty of Chinese women.

Below, a marble boat, its capstan ever ropeless, holds in the heave of water of No-Name Lake, unrocked.

Roy Gridley

Wine Spring in Gansu's Gobi

The rails zipper shut as they recede.
Finally, out the window, a human form,
the first in twenty miles: a bundled
figure hunched upon a yak cart heading
south across dry flats dusted by snow
ribbed with sand shaped into wakes
downwind from sparse thistle and sage.

I guess he's got someplace to get to,
some hut, family, flock, work beneath
the petty shelter of Qi Lian Mountain.
Maybe he'll have gotten there when I
step off at Jiu Quan Station to ponder
General Ho who long ago laced this spring
with wine and worked his desert miracle.

I buy a bottle of wine still endorsed
by the General, lean back on a mud wall,
take a gulp, stretch, smoke, squint south-
ward into the winter sun, cold and silver
as the moon. Qi Lian Mountain hazes out.
I gulp again, sigh, long for the cozy
landscape of Dodge City, Cheyenne, Amarillo.

Roy Gridley

Desert Music

A breeze works its way down
along the elms and willows
lining Da Quan Creek. Banks
of cantilevered ice stretch
to bridge the clear shallow
water cutting across gravel.

His beat now shadowed cold
by the caved sandstone cliff,
the guard stomps one last time
across the bridge, claps frozen
gloved hands, checks his watch,
strides off–out into the dunes:

machine gun slung over his right
shoulder; on his left, catching
sun in rich wood-grain, a lute.

Tongue-Twister for Sally

Clearly calligraphed electric
transmission pylons march
straight across the River Li.

Below, six gravestones, loomed
over by high, rounded peaks,
face limestone cliffs streaked

by bold, black brushstrokes.

Roy Gridley

Waking

The soft ruminations of Bezoar of Ox fading
high crenellated walls of sleep collapse
clickety snake of dominoes
dark ivory on white enamel
puffs the yellow dust
toward the wisp-bearded one
crying
He Forsook the Fears of His Fathers and Followed
through the gates of ears
snap snappity snap
plastic pistol
pa-chow pa-chow
a tight-voiced child
executes his only friend
long ago long ago
beneath the twisted pine
beyond the cotton-clogged screen of my window

Jim McCrary

Untitled 7/25/91

Thinking about out there
the clouds gather
push east and south
to here
where hopefully they will
do what they do
covering both sun and land
with the mass of them

some electric
some noise
a bit of wet
then move on toward the
easy hills of west missouri
or simply dissipate and
reflect above the kansas river
where i can see the loss

Not much else is there
i say to myself
and that is good
conversation.

Jim McCrary

Untitled 3/18/92

When the will comes
there are no fields left
trees line the banks
upended by the winter
ahead of this view another line of rock
road perhaps or simple lift
somewhere out there
a "how you say" mirage
visiting scenes from over by there
only in mid-day
only in mid-summer
only here on this hill do they visit
"you can see it as clear as day"
hopefully this is a chance
there is nothing to feel
go ahead walk through it
turn around and it is gone
somewhere nothing has changed
as usual this becomes the day.

Jim McCrary

Untitled 7/26/91

Under the horizon
a simple tree line
reflects
both heat and a few stray
head.

Before that a pond
both stark and quiet
which holds a few bass
and endless reflections.

To one end the constant windmill
dribbles what is left beneath it
in an ageless attempt
to keep up.

West of course the yellow
turns red and lights up what's
sent from topeka to pollute the edge.

i can either stand still or walk
back down the slope
or across the slight valley
called Buck by some
trying again to locate
what it is draws me here.

Always looking
always close
the only way here is subtle
and that is not an easy way
to get past.

Jim McCrary

Address Unknown

(1)

It was probably the first portable phone I'd ever seen. Pay phone it was arching through the door of the North Side Saloon. Pay phone. By chance landing in the back of Orville Young's International flatbed as he passed. It would lay on the hay straw overnight in his shed. The phone had been launched by Ludi Allen in a bit of frustration into the mid-morning minimalism of Oskaloosa, Kansas. I was sitting in a booth enjoying a 2nd red beer. "Hippy Jim." This was a few years back. It was Ludi. "Take me down to Sporty's." That would be another beer joint 10 miles due south on a line with Baldwin but short of and on the bank of the Kaw river. That we did. All this has happened before.

(2)

Ludi Allen was 8th generation Kickapoo. Lived with her 82 year old dad just south and a bit east of Oskaloosa. George Allen was my closest neighbor. A champion dancer and a widower. He wore his deceased wife's pig tails when he danced and carried a sawed-off 9 iron affected with a horse tail. George Allen Senior so as to separate from George Allen Junior. Sonny. Ludi's older brother. It was Sonny's wife christened me "Hippy Jim." Lisa Allen was 4th generation white. She was a patient woman who could make a person feel awfully comfortable–simply. Sporty and Cleta were carnival folk who in the midst of retirement purchased THE WELCOME INN. PERRY, KANSAS. ELEVATION 850. They too could make a person feel comfortable–simply.

(3)

The first thing caught my eye in Oskaloosa some four/five years earlier was a sign on the court house door hand written pre felt tip pen it was: EARS $2.00 EACH. Made no sense to me yet announced to locals that bounty was in effect for Coyote extremities. Not much visible ears or no except still quaint folklore which held that dead Coyote attached to barb wire fence would keep away others of ilk. George Allen Sr. had a pair of Grey hounds and a night's entertainment was to turn them loose and listen. Grey hounds chased Coyote and vice versa. Very much hill and dale. It was definitely a multi-media event. The way it was–usually after midnight–George wearing seed cap and top coat past his knees laughing at the bark and hoot taking place. "There just north of Bud's place running toward Tongie." And they did. We'd sit, listen and then he would go on home. I never have come to understand how any of the participants knew when to stop for the night.

(4)

Thunder bolts the size of silos danced around us as we motored over to Perry. "Don't worry," says Ludi, "the tires keep us grounded. Lightning can't hurt us." Looking back in a 90's kind of way I see that was a classic case of denial. The vehicle was a '59 Dodge Dart convertible. As well, as well, a fine example of Kansas Magic Realism.

(5)

All this waiting for a bus on Fillmore St. The past past like that opaque dawn mist over a farm pond alongside the Wellman Rd. coming down the sweet slope of east Kansas.

Memory pulled up then gone into the full sun of another day.

Trish Reeves

Collect Calls

I become one of those people I've overheard
making calls from pay phones:
a woman untwisting the cord with her fingers.
She sometimes cries and
even though I'm not crying, I am
the woman on the phone
and the line feeds to a dark kitchen
below sleeping children
where a man whispers: I kicked in the bedroom
television tonight because the woman I love
most of all after you
plans to leave town. Call me
sick enough to hurt myself, he says.

I tell him to please speak up,
I know he's strong enough for this.
I untangle my right hand from the cord
and reach to finger the holes
in the dial. I'm standing in a corner
of a kitchen full of people at a party.
I know these people,
I know they're trying not to listen.
But the only form I see is his—
straight through the receiver,
a man framed by a black circle.

Trish Reeves

Pure and Rapid

The big dead tree burns
from the inside out.
The farmer filled it with kerosene
and now the chicken hawk and farmer
watch the fire. Chicken hawk
sitting on a new tree,
farmer standing close enough
to feel the heat the hawk
won't touch.
Hawk, farmer, neither
wish for gentleness
while they stare at the invisible
turned sharp shapes and colors.
The hawk thinks of the rough rust
coat of the heifer, the prize
that's too big for him
that he's certain is full of blood.
The farmer thinks of the room
above the strip-tease in town—
nothing in the room
but light from the neon tube
shining the walls red.

The air around the tree
knows the hawk and the farmer.
But like them, feels only the fire—
pure and rapid
radial pain.

Trish Reeves

Dark Chopin Tie

I'm sitting on the couch listening
when my daughter walks in.
She asks me if I'm listening to Mozart,
she tells me the mother across the street is listening
to Mozart. I'm listening to Chopin.
I hold up the plastic CD case
to show my daughter the picture. Chopin, I say.
I know little
about this kind of music but that to listen to it
helps. And then I'm startled, I see the dark brown eyes
of Chopin, the erratic cut of hair.
I stop myself from saying:
He looks like your father,
doesn't he look like the man I divorced today,
the man I was married to at 11 am,
the man I divorced at 41,
the man who was not there for his no-fault divorce
in Court 13 on March 13th. The divorce
that was followed by
three other women in line
for no-faults before noon.
Mozart, Chopin
the three women behind me in Court 13,
I trust them: the women would say
my husband was actually there this morning,
they had sensed him in his white collar
and the Chopin tie
just as I.would have to say
I sensed their husbands,
through it was their absence
that explained the women's lives to me
like music.

Trish Reeves

The Dark Birds

three of them,
learned in their mother's bodies
how to perch so high
on a slender twig
atop a bare tree. When the wind
keeps everyone inside, when the ice
gives form to the wind, the dark birds
nevertheless can be seen, standouts
sitting the insubstantial
forty, fifty, sixty feet up. They know,
inside the dark shine of the cap, a small bit
about the wonder in the eye
of the onlooker, a bit more about
the ability to balance on nothing, and everything
about the price they will pay, over
and over in sinew and strain, for the rise, the lift
from nothing to the moment.

Trish Reeves

Guisborough Shore

> *Turner's title merely means: drawings*
> *done on the shore while staying at Guisborough.*
> Gerald Wilkinson

Brushing in the trees
rather than breathing them in:
this is life. Always a little more
water, and a little higher
water in the background. With notes
above the mountains and the clouds.
What does it mean
that Turner's mother was mad,
that the Royal Academy named him
Professor of Perspective,
that the professor's favorite word
after "light" was "doubt"?
It means nothing.
It means the world is made out of paint:
that the woman in the museum
who studies the blue wash of genius,
the paper with the crease down the center,
wishes to refold the sea,
take it home
and keep it in her heart, her storm.

James Bogan

Virtuous Amusements and Wicked Demons

by Ch'en Chi-ju
Resident Fellow Confucian Institute of Correspondence
Ming (i.e. luminous) Dynasty
from his greatest work: the *Shu Hua Chin T'ang*

I.

Of Virtuous Amusements, i.e. good conditions, are numbered the following:

a party of articulate lovers
a clean table
the season of tea, of bamboo shoots, of watermelon
a host who is not bold and severe
reading a great book slowly
sitting in the midst of landscape paintings
burning incense and cultivating fine manners
examining old masters
no need to close the window
a great monk in the snow (i.e., philosophical discussions)
to be surrounded by rare stones, wild flowers, hand-made vessels
recovering from illness
walking to the River
dry shoes
snowed in with friends
plenty of time to roll and unroll the pictures
strong men and sublime music
a clear sky with a beautiful moon—
or as Snyder's Bojang puts it:

"On top of Cold Mountain the lone round moon
Lights the whole clear cloudless sky—
Honor this priceless natural treasure
Concealed in five shadows; sunk deep in the flesh."

II.

Of Wicked Demons, i.e. bad conditions, are numbered the following:

the unwilling horse
the season of yellow prunes
after drinking
inscriptions written in a confused way
a hurried visitor at one's side
too busy to watch the sun set
a room where water is dripping in
cares of the world
sneezing rats
to ask the price
pictures used for cushions
eaten by bookworms
sad dreams in a fitful night's sleep
a handle that does not fit the socket
aching ears (i.e., idle talk)
broken shoe-laces
a hundred degrees in the trailer

III.

(Ch'en Chi-ju goes on to distinguish the good and bad fates that may befall a painting)

Here follow assorted bad fates which may befall a painting:

to be scorched in a fire
to fall into the hands of a jerk
to be pawned
to be buried in a tomb
to be covered by glass
to be cut up for roof patches

Here follow assorted good fates which may befall a painting:

to be hung near a window at eye-level
to belong to a literary courtesan
to be placed in a sturdy frame
to be named well
to be admired by opened eyes
to be painted by Fan Kuan, Raphael, Tom Benton

IV.

Ch'en Chi-ju's last words:

From the grapples
of Wicked Demons
into the hands
of Virtuous Amusements,
Kuan-yin
Deliver us.

James Bogan

Jonah's *Last Wish*

"A chemical being is shielded from the lethal weight of creation
by a natural unreceptivity, by callouses, epidermis, and obliviousness."
Richard Grossinger in
The Long Body of the Dream

"I saw the open maw of hell,
With endless pains and sorrows there;
Which none but they that feel can tell—
Oh, I was plunging to despair."
Jonah

"When down in the mouth, think of Jonah; he got out of it."
Thomas Edison

• • • • • •

Well
how do you suppose
Jonah felt?—

Shrieking wind whirls calm surface
to raging vortex
Storm-twisted timbers groan
to match sailor's moans

Then having jettisoned
reams of purple silk
casks of red wine
and an order of gold amulets
His mates toss him overboard
to purge their bad fortune.

(Do you suppose
as they grappled and heave-y-oed
him squirming
that one son of Poseidon said:

"Sorry, chump, but it's one of you
and all of us."
Or—
maybe on three:
"Bon Voyage stranger!"

The curling sea swallows the shy prophet
til he surfaces
choking out brine
saying his prayers

No time to jiggle water out of his ears
No time to rub a bulwark-banged head
No time to fret the sinking passport

And HERE is the Space
Ryder shows
in American vision
down the line
from Rembrandt
& Turner

WHEN Jonah's last Petition
comes answered
in the prodigy
of the monster-fish

Death agony doubles
arms that should swim
recoil in fear
tormented eyes reflect
exchange of drowning-doom
for terror of being eaten alive
sliding in mauled pieces
down the long gullet
of the slimy whale.

(("Give me the peaceful suffocation of drowning,"
he had said a Year and a Day ago
considering fate theoretically
sipping heated brandy
dry feet on the fender

of the Superior wood stove
cosy
in Joppa's friendly Lighthouse Taberna.))

Meanwhile,
shining through the black sky
and whited waters
a bearded *deus ex coeli*
blesses the scene

As Jonah
screams
chokes
spits
screams
his way
to salvation
and Nineveh

Whereupon the ship-safe seafarers
gasp in horror
and exhale relief.

Philip Wedge

In Retrospect

Once, during our year of separations together,
you went out to dinner with another man
who wanted to be more than just a friend,
and out on a walk, trying to forget where
you were, or what you might be up to
(not to mention what he might be up to),
I found myself in a street with no
access out, in front of a restaurant
queue and the two of you approaching.
At first I tried to hide beside the wall;
then, like scared game hemmed in by
beaters in a wood, I bolted up the street.

As a boy my fear was more generally
felt, like at five when I cycled
into town, proud to be on an errand
alone, but ended up in the wrong place,
determined not to let others know I was lost.
I was sure their looks were on my neck
if I suddenly changed course illogically,
the logic of the lost. At times I feel
it still, embarrassment of turning back,
but not to you, not to you.

Philip Wedge

Van Gogh's "Crows Over a Cornfield"

(*Nelson Art Gallery, 1963*)

Not the polished, medieval armor,
gape-mouthed, empty in the entrance foyer,
nor the moon rising in chinese tapestry
over wooden bridge by high mountain,
but the skeleton crows held in mid-flap
above the cowering wheatfield;
the scraped-on yellow whistling from the canvas
just as at home it would in a world already
over-familiar to my eyes till seen suspended
thus, as if it awaited my stopped-breath
seven-year-old wonder to bring
it back to life... crows criss-crossing
still, wheat ready for harvest and barely
time enough to get it in to dry.

Philip Wedge

The Sandpits

A red-red setter blunders forward
through brush to the water's edge,
my setter, but no more a part of me now,
than me a part of the city we have left.
A cold, Sunday morning
and hunting season's come to boot,
but my hands are deep within
their rust-coated pockets
and my untrained red, rust-red setter
raises an instinctive paw,
barks an alert to all hunter-waiting prey.

(Somewhere, my father will raise a gun-salute today
at blue-winged teal, or slow-poke mallard,
for he has switched religions now,
and shotguns *are* better than booze.)

This is no wild country place, here,
just an ear-shot from the interstate;
but it does have its solitude.
The dredging crane leans in still silence,
poised to stir again the clouds of sand below,
but there's no use for sand-dredging now.

The setter splashes her way clumsily on;
she's no longer my red, dust-rust, red setter,
but a sleek coot-hunter—a head-bobbing red otter.

Thinking of quicksand patches too late,
I try to call her back,
but she is the thought given expression now,
and she voices her own will.

Grown tired of the useless chase
(for no one said coots can't swim),
she pants a dripping trail to my bank-perch,
shaking,
rolling like a horse in the dirt, the leaves.
Her search, my search, has come to nothing,
dust, dust, dust-red setter.

Philip Wedge

Car Keys

We shared the same childhood, almost the same;
yet events you learned well I soon forgot:
the night you hid the keys from father, when
he was drunk and mother screaming him not
to go ... *that* night he broke his foot on some
fresh-turned gravel; no one could believe the
story ... but somehow I forgot all that,
except the gravel, who could? You held it
in your mind vividly and let it spill
out just as then, fifteen years further on.
I drink like Dad; you scream like Mom.
Which one of us holds best our childhood?
So often I could shut those hard times out
from the picket-fenced backyard where we'd play
with the dog while you stood in the kitchen
watching our parents fighting over keys:
keys to Dad's illness, keys to Mom's sadness.
My key was tomorrow: tomorrow we'll
grow up and leave; tomorrow *be* all right;
tomorrow Dad won't need long walks at night.

Brian Daldorph

Dads With Kids

Sunday mornings it's our turn,
after getting away from them all week.
New men all,
surrogate mothers,
we take our kids to the park,
pretending
we'd rather not be home
watching the big game.
While kids run crazy
as footballers without
rules pads helmets
trying to hurt themselves,
we exchange words—
not the easy chat
we have with skilled young mothers.
But there are the college frisbee girls
twirling in the sun,
watching, we think,
being good dads,
college girls who, perhaps,
go for older men,
men they dream are good with kids
every day of the week.

Plummeting Upward

I'm a man on the rise,
plummeting upward
with my concrete wings
iron bones
and symphonic song,
up up up till
I'm buried
in sky.

Anne Wallace

An Alchemy

Into the space of another's breath. Tasting.
Skin cedary and warm,
a third body, passed
without resistance.

All day long the ear
empties, sound spilled
into pumping veins, and slowly
refills. A bird's one note.
The refrigerator's hum. Separate
breaths.

Sitting on the floor in the late light, not seeing.
Green light filtering through striped screens,
chameleons' quick shadowed runs. Not seeing, seeing
what has changed.

Anne Wallace

Measuring

First they compare hands.
His just lap hers.
The second bone of her little finger curves
like his.

Then he tries his arm against her back.
When he lays his elbow on one shoulder-joint,
his wrist rests on the other.

They lie down face to face.
Their bodies nearly match in length.
Her belly fits into his.
Her hands reach his hip-hollows.

All this time they talk. He works thought
like a jeweler, meticulous in his words.
She pours herself out like a river, knowing word-shapes
only as she speaks. They hear their minds cross.

All the time they find more.
Wine seeks the same level in their glasses,
the wooded hills of Ohio remind her of Kansas.
When he lays his palm in the curve of her cheek
his finger-joints just find her brow.

This will take a long time, there are so
many pieces, such odd shapes.

They lay their lives together. They keep
measuring.

Anne Wallace

First Eyes

This must be what she saw with her first eyes
before she knew the word "prairie" or could name
the blue behind long white November clouds.

Wind rises from fields where a man is plowing,
opening the earth to winter wheat.

On the hillside, where farmland lapses into grass,
other men work near her coffin,
covering raw black dirt with green rugs.

We stand in the cold wind, each knowing
we see this scene as she taught us,
respecting winter, not turning from the open grave,
watching a single hawk
stooping through the clouded light,
grass drying where it stands.

Anne Wallace

Photos: November

All of us behind the grave,
sitting and standing in two lines.
Crossed hands, sunglasses.

My brothers walking with our grandfather,
each poised on one foot,
hands pocketed, coats blown.

The coffin balanced
on the horizon, its wood
grass-brown.

My hand holding her head. Her hand
clutching her sunglasses. Our faces turned away.

What we never saw
remembered.

Anne Wallace

Like Bridges Spanning

Hadn't he thrown himself
            across that abyss,
launched his body through
            the long days between?
Hadn't he found another body there, not
            the one he expected?
Didn't it feel like a cable, a pylon, a pillar?
Steady, strong, sunk into muddy bedrock,
stretched out across into
            a different body, there.

            And so we are like bridges,
not like animals or angels or even like ourselves
but bridges spanning,
arching out
toward unseen arms
that bear us up
            before we know we've fallen.

Anne Wallace

500 Locust Street

with accompaniment on sketch pad and pencil

This is just one sound.
While they draw music plays, feet move,
the heater turns on and off, trains come in standing waves.
But this is the sound that points to this place.

The model's foot rocks a bit against the platform.
It is hard work, she sometimes shows the strain,
but holds herself relaxed.
Her feet press down on the smudged white wood.
If she moved it might make this sound.

Long slow looks, long lines pressing
white paper. Up, their eyes,
and down and up,
glances crossing and recrossing where she stands,
arms arcing along the eyes' line.
Intent as prayer, brushes in
their mouths,
they forget their bodies. Everything falls in toward
this place.

This sound. The linked rhythms of common work
focus here.
Standing where she stood I try to draw a line, one line,
this line.

Mary Klayder

Reminders

1957

Why did you buy me this damn
planter? I want personal
gifts. No one ever buys me
personal gifts.

1961

Why did Mrs. Stewart think
you copied that drawing?
Didn't you tell her
that you drew it yourself?
Doesn't she know
you can draw?

1966

If he's not here
in five more minutes,
you might as well change
clothes and watch
a movie with me.

1971

Go back to the apartment
and get my earrings. They're
on the dresser in the pink
box. You'd better hurry
if you want me to look
right at your wedding.

1978

My daughter is a
schoolteacher. She's
really good with kids.
She takes after me.

1985

So when did he start
stepping out on you?

1987

I hope you finish
that degree before
I'm dead.

1988

You know how proud I am
of you. I worship the ground
you walk on, well, not the
ground, but you.

1989

I know I can't talk
as well as you
but you know
what I mean.

Mary Klayder

> In ancient Egypt, Thoth, the god of writing and knowledge,
> was frequently depicted as a baboon.
> *–placard at Oriental Museum University of Chicago*

Baboon

Swinging freely from side
to side, its rhythm builds
between my ears. An image
darts upward, blurs,
bolts past my right
eye. A sudden drop
to my throat, it pauses,
waits, feeding upon air.

Then bolts again upward,
slows, climbs behind
my left eye, hides
silently, waiting,
gone.

A sudden bound up
and again
it drops,
sits, crawls cautiously
forward, then
leaps.

I utter ape-thoughts.

Mary Klayder

Morning Conversation

My words,
like oatmeal, sit
in bowls, waiting
for cream and sugar

His words,
two crisp strips
of bacon, drain
on paper towels.

Philip Kimball

breaking the plains

it's not the tractor in the fog,
the faint percussion in the middle ear, muted and dispersed,
popping Johnny's progeny, john deere's plowbeam, soil-polished plowshare,
twelve bottom moldboard suited to the plains.
soothing reassurance, stitching air and land, an earthy first fragrance
permeates, loess and loam, gasoline, oiled gunny, sweat and rain.
it's not the moiled light that intervenes, gleams and saturates
the steel, paint and plastic, the wet windshield glass of toyota, audi,
volvo, suburu, chevy and ford parked along the right of way,
the barbed wire fence row of the old oregon trail, where the heavy wagon box
clatters and twists, the loaded axletree and iron-wrapped wheel,
canvas canopies slap, strain and stutter, travel,
jangled chain over ruts, cattle, an ox, a spotted hog in tow.
it's not the gravel road that cuts north along the edge across the draw,
the dormant switch grass and wild rye that grow in the ditch, crinoidal
limestone shards, mollusk matrices, the sunflower stalks
that will ravel, rattle and blow, the indifferent bois d'arc hedge
spreading tangled offspring into the field.
it's not phlox, sand dropseed, prairie gourd, goldenrod,
mead's milkweed, the fringed orchid, purple clover, queen anne's lace,
squirreltail, needle-leaf sedge, pussy toe, redtop and daisy fleabane.
it's not the distant talkers, the nikon shutter, discussion,
testimony, witness and the awe. it's not john brown, jim lane, quantrill,
speculators, sod busters, border ruffians, jayhawkers,
molasses lappers, exodusters, clod hoppers, not
buffalo, fox, antelope, puma, prairie dog,
mastodon, teleoceras and sabertooth cat.
it's not the kaw.

it's the phantom self-consciously stripping bluestem spikelets to carry home,
the spectre in the mirror, the pucker and fold
around the wary green eyes, the well-fed flesh year round, kumquat,
cantaloupe, kohlrabi, artichoke, brown rice, tofu, lox,
pork chop, bacon, leeks, kale and beans.
the face, the curls, the nod, the wistful grin, the deprecatory frown,
protruding ears, the yellow teeth, dull skin growing taut
about the pale forehead, the cheeks and jaw, the chin, the closed skullbones
underneath. frail, transitory. exposed furrow ribs. orogeny,
alluvial deposits, eroded and washed,
uplift, thrust and fall, settle and fill.
it's you, caught up in this inexorable turning.
not the landscape will not survive, the ocean gone, but you
evolving to the dust that swirls from shears and scatters
in obscure morning mist.
you drifter in the prairie flux, desperate seizer
of an imaginal razor now.
let loose. you turn the sod.
it's you who drive the plow.

Philip Kimball

Two Plagiarisms from Rilke: fragments from forlorn days

...like birds grown used to going
and become heavier and heavier like falling:
the earth sucks from their long claws
the bold memory of all
the things that pass
and makes them almost leaves which hold
close to the ground,—
like plants that creep, stunted, into the soil,
sink into black clods, pale
and soft and damp, and sicken,—
like children lost,—like a face
in a tomb,—like hands
become uncertain at distant reflections that quicken and roil
the surface loom of wine in a glass—
like a cry for help confronted
in the evening wind by the dark pealing of many large bells,—
like cut flowers wilted in a room,
like narrow streets in a bad part of town,—like locks of hair
in which strings of pearls are tangled,—
like morning in april
outside the many windows of hospital cells:
the patients crossed to the edge of the chair
to look: early sun
makes the park springlike and wide;
they see the light
turn blocks of houses young and trim
and do not know that throughout the night
storms tossed the sky,
storms of water run where the world's ice,
that storms still blow through the streets
that will relieve them of the burden of things,—
that something out there is large and grim,
violence out there, a fist
that would strangle every one of them
in the middle of this brilliance they believe.—
...like long nights in a withered bower,
the canopy warps, the lathworks twist,

and never near enough to cry in,—
like moon-bleached bones,
like naked girls coming over stones,
like drunks in a birch tree grove,—
like words that make no particular sense,
yet go into the ear, further
into the mind and clump in the nerves,
endeavor to jump and lurch through all your limbs,—
like an old man who curses his kind,
then dies so no one could ever
prevent the fate he deserves,
like full roses, artificially grown
in a blue hothouse where the air deceives,
wantonly thrown out in a large arc of bouquets
that lies in drifted snow,—
like an earth that never spins
because too much death weighs it down,
like murdered boys in a shallow grave
whose hands stave off the roots,—
like a tall, slender, red
high-summer flower
that suddenly dies in the gentle wind on the heath
because its root beneath
has struck turquois
in the earring
of a dead
girl's corpse...

and the hours of many days were just like this.
as if someone somewhere formed my likeness
to slowly mishandle it with pins.
i felt every prick of his play
and was as if a shower fell on me
in which all things transmute.

Philip Kimball

The island of the sirens

when he talked to them
who were his hosts, late,
in the evening, quietly, because
they asked about his travels and the danger:
he never knew
how to frighten them, with what sudden
word to move them so they, like him
in the blue becalmed island-sea,
could see the gold burnishing of those islands
whose viewing made the danger turn;
for it's not in the roaring, not in the raging now
where it always was.
Soundlessly, it overcomes the sailors
who know there's singing sometimes
on those golden islands—and lean blindly in their oars
as if surrounded by the stillness
that contains the entire scape
and drifts·about their ears
as if its other side
were the song
no one can withstand.

Philip Kimball

Boloney

Not gonna give up
my dogmeat sandwiches now.
It's ritual
food, along with Campbells
tomato soup, toasted
cheeze, slum
gullian and meat
loaf with some corn on the cob,
a baked potato and a big gob of cow butter.
And nothing better to eat
than pinto beans and chedder. But
they've poisoned dogmeat you say? Like
pox in the Black Foot and Big Belly blankets?
Monosodium glutinate, sodium nitrite,
erythorbate, glucono delta lactone? That shit
won't stop me.

Whole wheat (I'll admit
the prototype used Wonder Bread which
only protected bodies 8 ways back
in them days. But now and then on real
hefty slabs of Mamaw Kimball's white bread) spread
on mustard or mayonnaise, slice or two
of dog (had to peel and strip
the rind between the teeth) thick
red onion, pick out a tomato from
the window sill reddened
from the garden green, salt, Mamaw Couch's dill
pickles, some of mama's chow chow or a touch
of Jess's horseradish make you bolt the table
roll over on your back in the side yard
biting at the grass.
A real Dagwood. And a glass
of milk too (why not: fresh from the
neighbor's cow yesterday, much
yellow cream). So tie into it
like you're fighting wild tigers: no
poison able to match
the good
it will do.

Stephen Bunch

Dog Days

The sea that left this place
dry & chalky
ages ago
returns every summer, and

Billie's singing from a phonograph
willow weep
for me
passes through the screened window upstairs
2 houses down, settles
on the ear
dense & languid as the air
when the pressure drops & even
the *tao* index is falling

heat waves in the eyes of
Cyrus the Dog
of Rhode Island Street
who lies in a heap
at the curb
on the seabottom
in the shade of a blue
Ford pickup truck and

Einstein's brain nods in
an alcohol solution in
a jar on a shelf in
Wichita, Kansas

while the Local Dog chews
on the neckbone of *platecarpus*

are you Serious?

nothing to do worth doing
except the occasional visit to
the catalpa
sniff
lift a leg
sniff again

this is the life

Inland, See

the scene
suspended
forget this terrain
is terrain, the lies
your father told you
the lies you told your son

see inland
under the skin of the river
the sandbar forming
water & earth confused
step back in this air
stand on the littoral
& see again

against that backdrop
which could be the sky
the sea
rushing back over
the prairie

Stephen Bunch

The Choice, *from Radioracles*

KOAM, straight from Pittsburg, Kansas
Braxton B. Sawyer's Radio Pulpit
& the latest hog reports & soybean futures
every hour on the half hour

"Mah *frenz*, to*day* it's the Cubans
here in Ft. Smith.
To*mor*row the government's gonna tell you
that you got to rent that little a*part*ment
      over your ga*rage*
to a *ho*mo*seck*shal *school*teacher
& his sodomite boyfriend
who works at that vegetarian restaurant downtown.

"I wouldn't eat *there*.

"Then some *judge* is gonna tell 'em
they can adopt a little *boy*

"just like *your* little boy

"& *that* little boy can go to *school*
with your little boy."

Turn the dial, they're everywhere. XERA, Del Rio,
where Brinkley sold goat glands
& Winrod the *Protocols*.

"Someone has put something *down*
for me.
I've lost my *nature* ..."

Dr. Dallas Turner, Ms.D., cowboy singer, evangelist, author of
From Cocktails to Christ, distributor of *Miracle Messenger*
Healing Oil,
fades into Led Zeppelin
& back...

"Are you crossed up, mixed up,
bound down? 'Brother Dallas,' you say,
'somebody has my name written down backwards,
somebody's burnin' candles against me.'"

Old movies turn through the American television,
new cars through the streets.

The Moral Majority speaks from a tape
turning in the small studio of XEG in Monterey.

"...lift 'em out of the bondage of darkness!
Open their ears!
Blow away the darkness!"

...with automatic rifles.
Where their tongues should be,
place ashes.

"Someone has crossed you,
your hair is falling out.
Something crawls in your stomach.

"You have a choice, my friend.
It's *holiness* or hell!"

& the holy ghost moves &
rotten teeth are filled with gold crosses.
Adam Smith's invisible hand
rests on the president's mother's Bible,
the last whale beaches itself
& the missiles tick in their silos.

Judith Roitman

The death of the Elkins prairie

To perceive twelve thousand year old prairie, this community of roots like trees
existing and not existing, transmuting, intertwined with humus
until there is no distinction, like fingers, like hands grasping
and now pulled apart, not like bread, like bodies
tied to horses, the high cry beyond hearing,
the searing presence of air. I think of Armenians in black dresses,
their native villages, how the Turks drove them over the earth like rain.
Or Jews in Prague, the thousand year old synagogue, the thick walls,
its level eye slits, the women crowded behind them,
how they went up the chimneys like smoke,
like the coal ash that falls everywhere in eastern Europe's winter
giving asthma to the children. In my dreams redwoods
talk to each other forever, as I walk slowly with John's father
who can not look up from the arthritis.
I dream of the moon rising and my mother lost
among the great sand dunes of the Brooklyn shore.
Gulls wheel overhead screaming for garbage.
In the grass like tangled hair—the wildness!—
a man, it could be anyone, pores through bluestem,
(the movement of ants through childhood)
he moves forward on his knees, the car has long left him,
his face, his probing fingers, we must be careful
not to leave a mark, as if the planet
balances exactly on this point, the tip of yellow sorrel.

Judith Roitman

Chalk cliffs south of Oakley Kansas

Through the wall of rock there is blue sky
and towards the horizon more rock walls
against the sky. Some places
you can see things like this everywhere
but here people will drive over a hundred miles
to see such things. I imagine a landscape filled with goats
and foil wrappers, but it's all so clean,
like Mars or Venus, or the sudden crash
of machinery starting in a house at night,
the repetition barely recognized, and the stranger
that you think you know. The mind superimposing itself
against the landscape. The man who's deaf with a deaf wife
and his little daughter hears everything. That's why
it's hard to remember which buttons to push when,
like grass poking through back home, or hair.
Out here in the bright colors it seems so clear just what to do
faced with this kind of sky and no-one around
and the rocks soaring overhead like gold. That's why
it's hard to get back in the car and turn the radio on
although sooner or later we all do it anyway.

Judith Roitman

First pantoum for my parents

When she wakes up, she does not fall out of bed.
Lying on her side, she bends her knees towards her chin.
Her feet fall over the edge and she sits up.
He puts slippers on her feet and holds her hands.

Lying on her side, she bends her knees towards her chin.
He walks around the bed to her.
He puts slippers on her feet and holds her hands.
Leaning on him she lets her feet touch the floor.

He walks around the bed to her.
She grasps his hands and puts her weight on them.
Leaning on him she lets her feet touch the floor.
She walks into the bathroom by herself.

She grasps his hands and puts her weight on them.
When she is standing safe he lets her go.
She walks into the bathroom by herself.
He stretches and breathes, lying on the floor.

When she is standing safe he lets her go.
Sometimes he lets her sleep very late.
He stretches and breathes, lying on the floor.
He doesn't know is he should wake her up.

Sometimes he lets her sleep very late.
The doctor said she shouldn't sleep too much.
He doesn't know if he should wake her up.
Eventually she gets going.

The doctor said she shouldn't sleep too much.
When she wakes up she does not fall out of bed.
Eventually she gets going.
Her feet fall over the edge and she sits up.

Judith Roitman

Second pantoum for my parents

It is a clear day in San Diego
They are on a bench in Seaport Village.
A banyan tree is behind them.
They are facing the harbor.

They are on a bench in Seaport Village.
My mother's coat is bright blue.
They are facing the harbor.
Kites are flying.

My mother's coat is bright blue.
My father is wearing a plaid jacket.
Kites are flying.
There is a Navy ship in the harbor.

My father is wearing a plaid jacket.
My mother pats his arm and says "handsome."
There is a Navy ship in the harbor.
There are sailboats in the bay.

My mother pats his arm and says "handsome."
My father feels conspicuous in plaid.
There are sailboats in the bay.
My son is climbing the banyan tree.

Judith Roitman

The shooting of JFK as seen in a still from the Zapruder home movie

He is leaning slightly forward, as if talking.
His hands are moving towards his throat, as if trying to make a point.
Jackie is turned towards him. Her arm is resting on the back of the seat.
John Connally in the front seat has turned backwards, as if answering him.
They are in an open convertible driving by a green field.
You can't see anyone else in the frame, as if they are driving down a country road,
three friends on a beautiful day, for some reason dressed up, you can tell they are wealthy.
You can't see the driver. Most of the frame is filled by the grass,
but you can't tell if it rises or not, it just seems to go on forever up the frame so that even the sky isn't visible.
Everything seems so still, like when you come across a photograph of your grandparents when they were young
and they all look so lucky.
There is no way to tell, for example, that the first bullet has just struck.
There is no evidence except for the finger pointed at his own throat, as if for emphasis.
This is not the bullet that would tear half his head off,
just the one that nicked his tie, maybe his throat, the evidence is conflicting.
In their postures they look so concerned for each other, Jack clearly the focus,
the way Connally has twisted in his seat, as if listening intently, the angle of Jackie's head,
the way she leans forward slightly, as if he is making a point in an important conversation,
and everyone wants to be sure to hear it exactly right.
The way Jackie has halfway turned her body towards him, her face fuller than we remember it,
Connally's cheekbone so clear and sharp, the front of his face in shadow.
Jackie's soft pink hat, the sun shining off the men's hair.

Judith Roitman

With the Bengali writer V. L. Socrates

The reality of the sleeping women going in and out of coma on either side of her mother,
their skin smooth over the bone, her own mother's skin puckered and slack with effort,
fingers swollen with water that won't move through blood any more, the tongue moving in and out
with breathing. The wheel clicks formula through the feeding tube, clicks and clicks,
it will click past death until someone turns it off.

"Barbara," said the Bengali writer V. L. Socrates, chuckling at the joke that was his name,
"let me take you away from all this.
What is the mystery in the consciousness shooting off in all directions
until it is deader than firecrackers on the lawn?
What is the mystery in the dispersal of the ways we organize reality
until there is to the dreamer no reality left, not even breathing, which happens anyway until it stops?
While voices cannot be shut off they do not belong to anyone nor can she tell what they are saying.
The cold water on her brow—what intrusion is this when we only remember what we allow
ourselves, the keys that fit into the locks of consciousness?
How can anyone know what's going on, so why be surprised that in extremis
we are so palpably unaware, the brain having shed its categories like skin?"

As he speaks he reaches for her hand but she is lost in her mother's hair,
smoothing and smoothing it as if the flaccid body were her child, saying
"it's okay, mom, it's okay' over and over to this woman whose brain is so filled
with clots that there is almost nothing left to tell her. Who can tell if she feels the hand
on her forehead or localizes the sensation, as babies are said not to localize pain?

George Wedge

Two Roads to Cho-Fu-Sa
For E.P. and Rihaku

Her letter came on a hard day,
Muggy hot, and the old men sought
To take advantage of his young
Good will, muddling his brain
With off-hand remarks that confused
The bargaining. Her words stirred longing
For simple things, no more demanding than—
Yet what conceivably can ask for more
Than—a child-bride hungry for her man.
Hardly more than a child himself,

He bade her come as far as Cho-Fu-Sa.
That night he set her letter's words
To rhythms of his heart and slept
As he had forgotten how to sleep
For many weeks. But old men clutched
At him in his dreams, muttering
Of promises unkept, and the miles
To Cho-Fu-Sa stretched, dreamlike,
To infinity. When he awoke,
He stayed an extra day, then two.

On the river, one of the boys
Tended the cookfire carelessly
While others slept and caused delays
For repairs, for replenishing
Supplies, for a sudden opportunity
To profit through an unexpected deal,
With an old man who fooled himself
Trying to outwit the youngster,
Who long ago had given up his fantasy
That bamboo stilts would make good horses.

She waited mournfully in Cho-Fu-Sa,
Where gardens did not empathize
And parrots went on parroting
As if clipped wings were, after all,
A harsher fate than tight-bound human feet,
Her sorrow not worth repetition.
Here, mosses were hard put to find
A sprouting place in hard unfertile ground.
Everything spoke eloquently
Of someone's hard and thoughtless heart.

Five days, a week and more before
She heard; then it was by letter
And not the man himself, the careless boy.
She left it on the table where it lay
Unopened, packed her things, went home.
When he returned at last, he found
An old woman's heart beneath her
Young and pretty face, one more tired
Old person hoping to trick him
Out of something he could not afford.

George Wedge

Nine Lyrics from Innerland: Mind As Image

I

Having turned our minds inside out, emptied ourselves
to feed on the nature of things, their splendid utility,
we take their power, give up the strength we had,
sit our overstuffed selves down, too late, to contemplate,
through the gap between two buttons on our shirt, the
central mystery remaining in our universe.

II

Somewhere in the lilac bush a Carolina wren
knowing its place in the universe, sings freely.

From the north porch, wind chimes respond.
It is a clear day in October and there is sun,

green grass, red and yellow maple leaves,
a white cloud or two and a blue sky. I

shall be inside all day, forgetful and busy
doing what people do who have found things

to occupy them. Tonight in dreams, I will imagine
I feel the wind, smell the earth, hear the bird.
in the morning there will be the same bitter taste.

III

Until there was you, I was a vacancy to let.
Anything that paid the rent could move in.
Music was a tic in the mind, a tapping foot,
my breath arhythmic, out of phase, after the beat,
while possessions made possession irrelevant.
Now, you have possessed me and I wonder where
everyone and every thing I sought have gone.

IV

You held my name cupped in your voice and let it spill
over me. I heard and saw and reached to touch
the fabric of you; our mutual thirsts were slaked
from invisible springs, and all the things of this world
got their names from the solitude of us two together.

V

Always inside there are two of us, two sets of places,
two ways of sensing all that can be sensed,
two immaterial breathings of the fragile air,
strengthening us because it is more substantial.

VI

All day today, a bluejay has cawed from lilac and mimosa. There has been rain and the sky hesitates
between blue and grey, brother against brother, hoping something will happen
to decide the issue. Always inside, listening to music
we have shared, I hear the cacophony of separation.

The jay will not jangle me, I am not waiting
for the unexpected moment of our world's collapse.
All worlds fall in upon those who thought them certain.
At the last, survival is the greater risk.

VII

There will be rain tonight and swift winds;
the chimes will fill our sleep with primitive music,
and we will waken, perhaps, to the sound of geese.

All living things that know themselves know home.

We alone of sensate things wander in wonder,
looking for what a tree has never left,
a bird, a fish, a bear knows how to find.

VIII

Trees that were rich as gold a week ago
are bare; the stubs where limbs have been cut or fallen
make my eyes ache. If it happened to me,
they say, I would feel imaginary pain
in the missing limb. Science is so smart these days,
foretelling what I will feel before they mutilate
because I am just another human object
on a gurney to move from inspection station
to amphitheater to recovery—or not.
Little better than they, I stand here watching
wind toss imaginary branches lush with fall—
it is a form of serenity, filling out the shape,
rounding things off to be true to what we are.

IX

I am not waiting until there is nothing to see.
I will capture this stormy sky, stand in its rain,
face turned up, hands cupped to catch the liquid
Helen Keller understood at her sudden birth
outside in a green world she could not see yellowing.

Stephen Addiss

To a Bach Cantata

salvatoris hodie sanguis pregustatur

Sits like a fish in a shop window,
reading. (The author stares back palely.)
Stirs, puts the book down.
   ...I wait for the Lord, yea my soul is waiting...
Eats. Bread is blackened, salt
brings tears to the mouth,
starch fills the belly, pads the tubes.
   ...soul is longing...
Monday was bad, now Thursday
on its haunches sniffs the wind,
decides and is decided.
   ...yea for...
Rhubarb for supper. (Cats eat and digest,
humans fill their mouths and slide it down.)
Mastication stops. Coitus between
bread and mouth is cut off.
   ......
Closes the window,
shits, a friend comes,
hat tossed in corner, talks of women,
   ...Here my soul is waiting for the Lord
   more than watchers that wait for morning...
of partytime, sprinkled hair
and hair, and hair,
hours belabored into statues,
time posed white-armed,
twisted into contrapposto.

Sits in the chair, pinched,
three dowels holding the back,
invading the flesh.
Elbow on knee, what will the next meal be?
         ...more than watchers that wait ...
Pert, she's pert. Obnoxious, pernicious,
pert. Imagines a pinch, chuckles.

...yea more than they who do watch...
Someone, enough. The burnt toast,
the bad cheese, the three-pronged chair.
Sleep, a pleasure not known
and loved the more.
...for the morning breaking...

(The two tastes are of blood and of marrow,
and of the marrow the balls have the sweetest.
As an unwelcome gift, or sculpted
in time or words or music, the ball marrow is the sweetest.
But after the night, blood is subtle
in the mouth, in the teeth,
rumination more than flavor,
a taste of blood for early breakfast.)

...yea my soul......breaking, for the ...

(A woman in the street
tells the soon end of the world,
tells again, but looking ahead
does not wait for us.
Who sees her, who are the watchers?
the passers are now by.)

Sits in a booth, reaches for a coin.
Sits in a chair and prepares for the next meal.
Sits and talks to the table.
Sits, washed, blooded, hungry, stuffed, excavated, still.
Sits,
until he can wait.

Stephen Addiss

Textile

What is gone
of you whose hands were so cool,
and is the channel gone where
your hair crinkled wet wind in the night?

What is gone,
when is the clear when?
We are stamped in gold on white cloth,
we are worn above still water.

Stephen Addiss

Longmen Grottos

The Longmen Grottos, carved from fine hard stone between 495 and 750 A.D., were once perhaps the most beautiful Buddhist site in China. Over the centuries, however, they were first defaced during Buddhist persecutions, and then looted to sell to Western museums and collectors. Now the caves remain a tourist attraction, but more than ninety percent of the images are either broken or missing.

Raining so long
a brash new waterfall bounces down
past empty niches
where sharply chiselled
slender Bodhisattvas
one meditated silently
before the swift Yi River

Raining so long
the tourists have left,
and the huge Tang Buddha
(too large to have been stolen)
sits brooding
over a wet courtyard
empty
but for one stubborn old woman
who still hopes to sell seven bottles of orange soda.

Raining so long
the river roars past the caves where
–of all the thousand images
once carved to bring peace
to the souls of nuns, courtiers, merchants, soldiers
and to their ancestors–
now only the damaged,
the smashed, the headless
remain, slick and glistening
It may be raining
in Europe and America
where perfect statues
sit in cases and on pedestals,
rest in changeless light and temperature,

never getting wet–
but here in Longmen
the ugly and misshapen lurk in their caves,
breathe with the wet and cold
welcome crows and sparrows
and listen to the river

Stephen Addiss

Emperious

Once upon our time
if some untutored Chinese merchant
had built his home in
modules of five and nine, nine and five,
he would have been slain.

Those proportions were imperial;
the emperor owned
not only numbers but also words—
no one dared to write
the character graphs that were his name,
even on sutras,
so Buddhist teachings were copied with
empty spaces like
lost teeth in their slowly smiling graphs.

The Emperor owned
purple and his ministers crimson—
one fine court artist
was banished for painting an angler
in a warm red coat.

The imperial dragon had five
clawed feet, plebian
dragons had but three, yet now local
Chinese restaurants
are at least royal or palatial,
and if we desire
to build in five and nine, nine and five,
no one will notice
but architects; emperors are gone.

Stephen Addiss

Do my legs walk?

Not as well as they run,
but they still hold up
shoulders, ears, and fingers—
my hip clicks and clunks
in its socket as I move

When they are gone,
my life will be flat
as an incised pancake

Please play it once
at 33 or 45 or 78
with lasers, needles, diamonds, maple syrup—
perhaps it will scratch out a tune,
clicking and clunking one last time

And then forget it
let it go—
my nose and elbows knew it long ago

Jane Hoskinson

Inanna: Seven Gates
For Jessica

None of the ancient stone
tablets say why Inanna chose
to descend into the realm
of devastation, but it's clear
she knew the risks.

You did not choose
your childhood, raped before
memory, but this descent,
the sacrifice of every hope
of an easy life, this you chose
by a simple wish: just once
a chance at sanity.

Inanna left her priestess
at the temple gate, guarding
her return. You left me
and a list of telephone numbers
taped to your bathroom door
and checked yourself in
to the psych ward,
refusing to come back
without the truth.

• • •

First they take your jewelry,
then your clothes, piece
by piece, lying in drawers,
hanging in shallow closets
just behind the lime green wall.
They drug you at the gateway,
strap you to the bed.
Down becomes up; dark, light.
The only way out leads deeper in,
and yes, he's waiting for you.

He takes your arm
in iron hands, crushing
your spirit like an eggshell.
You cannot move or speak.
He drags you into the depths,
forces you to stand
where you can see your body
after he's finished with you,
hanging from a meathook.
He steals your name.

• • •

You take more names
than hell can hold. Some
scream their anger at your
lovers and friends.
Some are too young to drive
a car. Some hold his knife.

Inanna binds them all in daylight,
takes them to the store, carries on
their conversations. Ereshkigal,
queen of demons, meets her sister
in the underworld
and picks loose the threads.

• • •

You were so pretty.
Sometimes they told you that,
but usually they took you
without looking.
They hurt you more when you cried.
He liked to watch.

You put on the name
that went with sex,
the lipstick and the eyeshadow.
You left human feelings
tied up in the trunk of a car.

• • •

He studied medicine
once. He knew a lot
about anatomy.
He liked to see your belly
swell a little before
he cut away your children.

• • •

Your brother bought
a Smith and Wesson,
kept it loaded on the nightstand.
When he heard the stairs
creak, he rose on his elbow,
leaning against your shoulder,
and pointed the gun at the door.

He died before you took this tunnel
back into nightmare. He won't
help you now.

• • •

Weep. Weep for Ereshkigal.
She groans from the pit
of her belly. She sobs
in the restroom at work.
She knows who you are.

You speak her name,
and saltwater aches
behind your eyes.
Underground
streams roar all around you.

No star shines here. No moon
gives light, but you can see
the rising path. Your dogged will
bears you through the abyss,
back to your room and back
to work on Monday, eyes
burning like the morning star
inside demon-ridden skin.

Jane Hoskinson

Faces in Type

The Gothics stomp across the page
in boots: "No frills on me."
Helvetica goes dancing
like Twyla Tharp, no waste motion,
plenty of energy and a certain grace.
Cadedonia, serifs proudly raised on high,
marches to "Pomp and Circumstance," and Baskerville
remembers linotypes.

I remember Gothic thirty-six,
handset in sticks for headlines,
spaced out with em quads,
every line held firm
with strips of lead—one point of space—
or wood—two points—
and quoin-keyed into forms.

My hands still hold
the imprint of the cases
locked in memory like the long
age- and ink-stained fingers
of women the color of daguerreotypes
sitting on high wooden stools
throwing back type
with a flick of the wrist
or composing letter by letter
as they set galley
after meticulous galley
of dingy eight-point type.

The *Independent* face was Baskerville.
My father reported, edited and set type
at a single stroke
sitting at the lino keyboard,
his pants cuffs starred
with splashes of molten lead from the Saturday casting.
Drawing from fine-honed memory,
his hands, their lines inked like a woodcut,
set out the story as he'd written it
inside his head.

My brother at age twelve
set his first head
from the reader's point of view.
Leaded, justified, inked and pressed
beneath a roller turned by hand, it clearly read,
"akepoT sekirtS odanroT"
He never lived it down,
nor in twenty years have he and I outgrown
the childhood sense
that under the skin of our soaped and pumiced hands
the blood ran black and viscous in our veins.

I still proofread cereal boxes, enjoy the stain
on my hands of newspapers hot
off the press, read kids' books to my daughter
upside down, and sometimes miss the sense
of the words as the faces leap
from their cases and dance
on the page.

Jane Hoskinson

Nova

Alone as a star,
she pushed
away my hand.
The amnion thrust
through her cervix,
waters burst across the burning
skin of her thighs
and the small head,
hard as a stone,
spread the labia
open and pushed
into my hand, stretching
for the first
breath, bright
in new lungs
as a point of fire.

Michael Johnson

Lunch at the Flamingo Club

Slow start. Couple of beers, small talk,
muted music, stage lights on low.

Place a little empty, you think.
Then meatloaf, baked potatoes, rolls,

bumps and grinds, woman on a pole,
out of nowhere a smoky sea

of men's faces. An hour of skin
struts by, and you must leave—just when

the bat-girl is about to reach
your table to do her bounce-bounce

number under the cape for you
and the regulars down in front

are tucking tens between G-strings
and whole-body tans, between bald

lies and minimal promises.
At the door you hesitate, trip,

and almost fall, sobering up
to the duties of afternoon.

Michael Johnson

The Ballad of the Jealous Lover of Lone Green Valley

Benton would always whistle when he worked.
You hear him in the fiddle whose bow seems
to skew the whole scene.
                                                  First the sinuous
rhythms hold you, then the colors, and then
the tale in that space between a man's hand
wielding a dark knife and a woman's hand
against her chest, faces frozen in loss.

Critics thought this was the Ozarks. It is
not—though still a paraphrase of somewhere
else.
            That yokel playing harmonica
is Jackson Pollock, who already dreams
his own hollows and bumps, spilled arabesques.

Michael Johnson

First Trip to the Zoo
For Lauren

All the strange life seems lost on you until
we roll your stroller into the domed world
of the rain forest and something takes hold:

flamingos. Balanced on long, stalky legs,
they stand almost like plants in the clear pool
below the waterfall, plump blooms of pink

flame amid thick tropical green. They preen
their feathers endlessly, balletic necks
slowly undulant, reptilian. You watch.

Daughter, I think you see yourself in such
beauty—floral, aloof, more difficult
as the manmade jungle becomes adult.

Michael Johnson

July 27, 1890

For Kathleen

After the gunshot
at Auvers-sur-Oise,
nothing focuses:
horizonless roads,
wavy yellow wheat,
a scatter of crows
into blue unease.

Eros

For Anne Carson

Bittersweet god
mad for that lost
half knucklebone,
love's *symbolon*.

Victor Contoski

Flute Music

Through the late March sky
promenade the stars of winter
saying their names to music:

Alnilam
Bellatrix
Elnath

Arneb
Adhara

The wind
from the Colorado border...

Our little sister
who died thirty years ago
in her mother's womb
is practicing
her music lessons.

Victor Contoski

The Kansa

1

The Kansa, wind people,
south wind people,
told their children The
Beginning.

The first man and woman
grew from earth on an island.
Water everywhere.
Many children came,
quarrelled with their parents
and made children of their
own
with no place to put them.

Then animals sprung from the
earth
the small ones, friends,
beavers, muskrats, turtles,
who dived into the water,
brought up mud
and built, earth on earth.
And the island grew.

2

Then trees poked out,
put forth leaves
that flew and became birds.

Grass grew on the land.
Deer came and buffalo
to be food and clothes for the
Kansa.

3

And ever the land increased,
grew rough, heaved, divided;
and man also divided.

Earth People
the first to pitch tents
who knew the season for
moving
and the season for waiting.

Thunder People
who soothed storms
by casting cedar leaves
into the campfire

and burned prairie grass
to bring rain.

Buffalo People
sacred to the shaggy beast
sought him in the hunt
and could not eat his flesh
until others had done.

Ghost People
the first eaters at funerals
who took horses as payment
from relatives of the new dead.

Each to his element,
each to his season.

4

And after many winters
the buffalo moved to new
pastures onto the plains
leading the wind people
westward

to the land of their name
the flat land that
remembered its past
that remembered water.

5

And the Kansa moved out
to the Great Plains of the
midwest
carrying their medicines,
their pipes and holy sea shells
to the Kaw River Valley.

There they lived
till white men found them:
Fool Chief by Big Soldier
Creek
Hard Chief by Red Vermillion
Creek
American Chief by Mission
Creek
White Plume by the
Wakarusa.

There they waited with the
buffalo
to be pushed south
toward the wind
of their name...

Victor Contoski

Black Stones

A man in darkness
dreams of stars

dreams
      hands outstretched
of feeling his way
      step by step
      up the dark marble
      of a narrow staircase

as I dip my right hand
thus

into a bowl
of black stones.

My fingers brush them
one by one

worry beads
beads of a rosary.

I will wash my hands
I will tell myself
among the innocent
as my white hand rises
like a shard of a moon
with two black stones

my gift to you
Valentine

one for your left eye
one for your right.

Stanley Lombardo

Dragons

The devil is sleeping on my office wall.
He has a troubled grin on his face
and is snoring under his snuggled stone wings
between a poster of Kuan Yin and a silkscreen
of the Great Buddha's green bronze head.

Buddhism has flourished only in countries
where dragons are honored.

                                        We are trying
to honor our dragons,
but they come to us as devils.

Strategic placement helps.

                                        This one sleeps sweetly
between deep wisdom
and the vow to save all beings.

Stanley Lombardo

Descendants

Instinctively seek the line of trees on the grass edge of the parking lot,
winter cottonwoods and osage orange, scraps of leaves and a little grass
to walk on a short way south down the hill, and even if you had gone blind
you could still raise your left arm in the night and point to Sirius
flashing photons into your fingertips, and that would be enough memory
to assure you she is gone, gone the way of Egypt, the way of all memory,
gone beyond the awakening a single tree or star could elicit
if you had the endurance to see them as absolutely present and empty
and resolved not to pass this trouble on to your descendants
walking in single file ahead of you down the hill and along the road.

Stanley Lombardo

Louis Armstrong and I Meet our Fate Among the Stars

Two portholes in the ceiling
of the craft formed black circles
crowded with stars. Louis Armstrong
and I looked up at them

he was singing in a soft rasp
O *didn't he ramble* and we
rose slowly towards the openings
Mr Armstrong on my right

and I passed through and turned
to help him with his shoulder

and we floated briefly
curled like embryos among the stars

and as I felt the vacuum suck my blood away
gurgling, I saw a baby's smile
spread across Mr Armstrong's moonlike face.

Stanley Lombardo

Distant Mountains

She is teaching a class on the history of the family
and I am watching her through the doorpane.
She sits sidesaddle on the edge of the desk
and her hands move like flowers
as she lectures. I cannot hear her voice.
Her hair is pulled back. When someone
asks a question she inclines her head
and her eyes shine. The silence is different.
I want her to look at me through the glass
but she is in another world and never looks
although it would be so simple for her
to turn her head in this direction
and see me standing in the hall outside.
This is how the dead look at us and yearn
and consider going into our minds
with the whispered thought
"Just turn a little in this direction
and look at me, smile at me just briefly,"
but never do, or try but cannot quite,
manifesting instead after desperate effort
as white butterflies in distant mountains.

Stanley Lombardo

Birds

1.

Grief was for Hecuba
like small birds troubling
the inner organs, breathed in
with the air, sometimes
sleeping, for each of her dead children
a pair of black wings
trembling against her liver.

2.

Plato thought the mind was like a cage
filled with birds: babies start
with empty cages and we put in a bird
every time we think we know something
and we can open the cage whenever
we need to remember something, catch
the bird, but it gets crowded and confused
the wings the flurry and of course the mess.

3.

David pulled her from the lake
remember her body slack on the pier,
the rhythm, hands on her ribcage
mouth locked over hers the sweet vomit
the breath won't go in won't go in,
spirit, breath, shadows beating away
over the water and into the trees
her small pained mouth her mother's
O my baby you've got to make it
and *jesus he'll kill me* in the soft rain falling

but only when she's in the ambulance
and undying on the respirator,
does her angry ghosthawk
return through the trees and
slam resentfully back into her chest.

Stanley Lombardo

On Translating Hesiod's *Theogony*

First of all was GAP, but then
EARTH, broadbosomed
        and a permanent, non-slip floor
for the deathless beings
who hold Olympos' snow peaks,
and over in a corner, musty HELL,
and EROS, beautiful in a superlative degree,
who unzips our limbs
and rides the broncos of our minds
jesus wouldn't you know it
he was there at the start

and by the end
Zeus has fucked most of mythology
into existence
and history is about to begin
and the poet is fumbling with the names
of Odysseus' bastard kids
tying up the loose ends,
goddesses lining up to get laid by mortals
one hand job after another
trying to end the poem

they should have all left it in their pants

Kathleen Johnson

Giorgio de Chirico's *The Delights of a Poet*

Witness this lost
hour in autumn:
light swallowed hard,
deep in shadowed portals.

On the horizon, a train leaves
its trail of pale smoke
in cloudless skies.
The searing clock fixes
its stare on a man in white who walks
away, his long shadow
a fountain.

The cool noise of water
dances in noon air.

Others have seen,
under dark arches, changeless stone,
this exact slant of sun, carried it away.

They too are ruled by time.

Kathleen Johnson

Farm Wife

In the farmhouse on long
Oklahoma days
she waits
for peaches and tomatoes
to ripen, words
in her head.
Plump love-apples
line two kitchen windows
while she skins peaches.
Velvety curls drop
into a pail,
pelting tin one
by one like rain
on the chicken-house roof.

Countless wedges
of angel food cake are cut
for her husband,
neighbors when they visit,
and the sunburned strangers
who help
with the wheat harvest.

Each Saturday,
wearing a dress, dark lipstick,
she drives red dirt roads
into town to sell
her cardboard cartons
of fresh eggs.

And twice a week,
she waters her multitude
of houseplants: African
violets, begonias, wandering
Jew, the tall rubber plants
and grape ivy while
poems lie in her
bureau drawer
and jars with handwritten labels
collect dust
in the dark fruit cellar.

Kathleen Johnson

Space

At dinner this evening
my eleven-year-old told me
that tonight the moon comes
as close to the earth
as it will
until the year 2005.

Now he sleeps
between walls postered with planets
luminous and beautiful as jewels.
From his bedroom ceiling,
the solar system dangles
on strings he carefully plotted
the autumn he turned eight.

Before bed, I stop
at a window, find
the gentle white eye full,
giving each moving cloud
its color. No stars in sight.
I stand waiting for
the day my son will move
away from me
like light leaving a room,
the lonely kitchen table,
the eternal quiet, all
the phantom memories falling in
to fill such vast space.

Though precious stones
orbit in darkness
farther than anyone can see,
I believe in 2005,
when astronomers are mothers,
we will know more
of black holes and infinity,
how the universe could grow and grow,
starting, as it must have,
so terribly small.

Kathleen Johnson

To My First Lover, An Auto Mechanic

This morning I woke with
the taste of you
in my mouth,
the familiar smell
of metal, motor oil
and Camel cigarettes
from the dark cab
of your pick-up
eleven years ago.

I've slipped you into
my bed again.

I've watched us
on my parents' icy porch
in the snow-flecked light
of a yard lamp, where
we said goodnight,
wrapped around
each other while
the neighborhood slept:
your mouth wet
on my neck, the chill racing
down my back,
your articulate
hands beneath my sweater, mine
pleased at your crotch, the rise
straining against denim,

my body charged
as a souped-up Chevy engine,
your tender blue eyes.

I still dream
of us, a mad tangle of warmth
in the cold, before
it all stopped

like a smashed new car,
still shiny, still tuned for power.

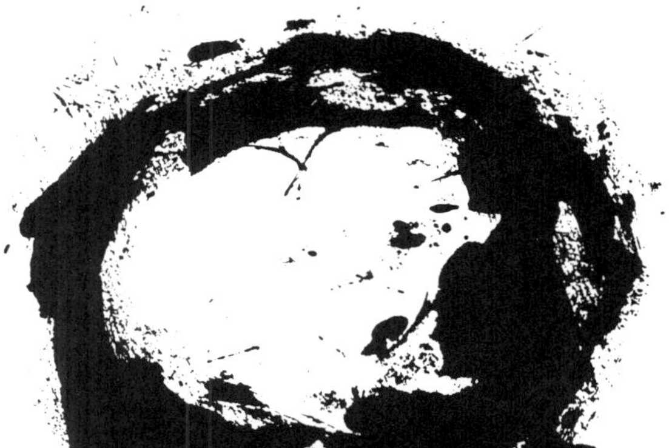

Karen Ohnesorge-Fick

Ma's Ghost

drifts near the ceiling above every head,
one Ma per son, daughter, and grandchild.

You have a yellow Ma,
Mother,
like a lightbulb in a cloud.
She's looking at you with a kind smile.
She's taking it and taking it.

With every Ma
there is a Pa to dish it out.
You have a yellow Pa,
Mother, floating with his wife
in the amphora of your wish
to hold them here
by taking it and taking it.

In your dream,
Ma and Pa eye one another with love.
Pa mows down her tulip bed.
Ma stumbles after on swollen legs—

together you chant,
you and your mother,
"Oh Pa, oh Pa, oh Pa..."

Karen Ohnesorge-Fick

Carriagemaker

Near Higginsville, in Corder
off a dirt farm road
shines a barn
covered in corrugated tin, the old wood
hid in siding.
More than a hundred years past,
my great-grandfather nailed each nail
in grief for hand-turned rails
and spindles of the crafted carriages
he'd made for wealthier Germans;
now, sinking a plow in new ground,
he'd found less than America's promise,
the dates curling away on his calendar
between him and homeland,
wires standing from his eyebrows.

Even now, in some remote villages,
the Chinese drape their dead
across the floor of an ox cart,
the woman crying, looking old,
the grandchildren circling at a distance.
They slap the ox across the back
till he lumbers off,
and magically,
when the ox returns for his evening meal,
the body is dislocated—
He made a little box, the dog
box, with dove-tail joints
and a hinged lid decorated with the image
of a hound in fragments of wood.

I forget my great-grandmother's name.
All left of her is the Catechism,
a Lutheran relic, printed in German,
the awkward sticks in human configurations
portraying the dramatic scenes,
hawks swooping upon them,
a crown laid upon a brow,
Adam and Eve loping out of the Garden,
the word of her son, who said,
this is the barn,
this is the box,
this is the book.

Karen Ohnesorge-Fick

Sleep Stages

My own mother is in the earth—
I hear her voice at night,
calling for a recipe, a better button-holer.

After her own dream, across a county line,
my mother-in-law feels the stiff waking,
when the eye of a stranger is still round,
when the fictive is odorless, but familiar.

That night when she wakes—
my mother-in-law—
she sluffs to the kitchen,
reaches into the dark for a glass,
feels for the faucet, lets
blast the sudden water,
and in the last cool
mouthful is a bristle of furled spider,
unalive and undancing,
but fluttering in the currents.

Marlon Ohnesorge-Fick

Canopy

In the center of your eye a new moon
spills the half-life of your past,
the evening train

as you screamed coming out of the house
(the cattle car & cattle car & cattle car
and now the oil and lime and 2 X 4s...)

until it dragged its tail into the trees—
delineations of the holy family
you should never have made—

your lid's corona
not knowing the end from the beginning—
the shoreline lost.

What could you, from the black backside
of a mirror, remember?
That time of year the leaves would naturally fall,
all that's dead in the west.
The burn of Kansas flour mills,
cicadas grinding at twilight,
good smell of bread loaves rising,
a loaf rising as a lung.

• • •

Mais en confusion, dans la brousse,
in October on Ogoue the handfires
burn back perimeter blight,

the bearded mange, like wise Chinese beards, and snake weed; the fires
flush birds that shriek on rusted hinges
through a dirty, smokey shroud.

Under umbrella leaves old men,
bent limb, cross legged, fashion their traps,
and children crack

under the flame trees
earth nuts between stones, and
women bail manioc from mud with sticks.

The earth is too fecund to breathe—
a sweetness
like a perfume bile.

Even the fish scent of new cut graves
is too heavy to float.

No cycle to death, no measure.
A number of blossoms on the flame tree exhaust themselves
in the presence of All There Is.
Tonight
the Bakota man
hitches a bronze gazelle to a bough
and with a linoleum knife spills its bowel.

The horns of the young bullmoose point back to earth,
the wet black nose to the stars.
The legs, snared leaping, nearly clear
the quarters cut away to be eaten.
It leaps into the night sky drumming its dead hooves.

I hear only the drumming now.
Feel only the heat of the fire and its dance—
a gyre of torsos whipped
by their own spines and hands, other hands–my own–our wattled fingers twining in Jacob ladders, our
feet just
leaving the ground.

Caryn Mirriam-Goldberg

Diana, the Huntress, Vacations in the Flint Hills

The hills sleep
like old dogs too lazy
to lift their heads.
Diana unties her robe and slips
her white feet into the delicate
mud under the water, nymphs all around.

As she lifts her cupped hands
to her wide, white face,
she sees him: an old farmer
looking for that crazy bull
who broke the fence again.

The farmer only sees a blur
of pink petals around a woman rising.
He figures it's worth a look.

Diana towers before him,
drops of pond water sliding
down her breasts, each as large as his head.
She waves her fingers to quiet the pink nymphs,
and before he can explain about the bull,
she thrusts both her palms to the sky
and turns him into a heifer.

Soon the bull finds the farmer
while Diana rolls on her side down
the hill, her butterflies after her,
letting each blade of bluestem
dry her perfect body.

Caryn Mirriam-Goldberg

About Desire

1.
Northern lights! So we grab the baby and run north. When we stop,
our breath hardening in the air, Ken says, we made a mistake,
it's only fog over the airport lights. But it's still amazing, he lies.

2.
In the good dream I lean my hands on the kitchen table where my
great-aunts eat cheesecake with cherries. I squat slightly. Now
labor can begin, but instead the baby's head crowns. I pull it out
by its shoulders and tell the aunts, it's a girl. Well, that was easy,
they say, but why aren't you wearing any panties?

3.
Even this far south, in our neighborhood once, with everyone
in the middle of the street, t.v. guides under their arms, pointing up
and staring, we saw the red flare across the stars. We saw it move.

4.
In the bad dream a man with food in his beard says, it's a miscarriage.
He spits tobacco on the floor, whispers, and it's your fault.

5.
Desire is like dust, the bodhisattva in the bathroom says. Put it in a
certain light and it becomes what you yearn for. Dust on the atmosphere
and you get northern lights, an illusion of the divine when really
god forgot to vacuum.

6.
Sometimes I go for walks with the baby and his stroller. While he points
to every light fixture and says, moon, I feed him the cherries I just
bit the pits from. He points to cats and laughs because they're all his.
We're happy.

7.
Once, almost asleep, I wanted a lover so much I invented one: tall,
muscular, brown hair and blue eyes, all compassionate so he weeps
into my hair for my loneliness. This is what Jesus must be like, I thought,
but then again, why not the best?

8.
I sit on the grass and cry. The sky is clear, relentless with stars, the grass dry and nosiy. Ken lays out his jacket and unbuttons his jeans. The first baby's asleep, he whispers, let's make another.

9.
In the worst dream I live alone in a tenement, eating soup from the can, cold, and watching reruns of The Beverly Hillbillies. I want nothing.

10.
When I get a fever I start to see things: last week the stomach flu made me lay down and watch flutters of white leaves fall. The train's whistle every half hour turned into an all-knowing animal who would answer any question I had of the universe. After all the aspirin in the house I still couldn't stand it so I got up and vacuumed.

11.
In the best dream of all I'm awake and can ask anything: what is god? may I have an orgasm now? am I pregnant? make cheesecake materialize. And the answer–always the same–is a picture of the planet with a red arrow pointing to a glob of green next to a sign flashing, yes, you are here.

Caryn Mirriam-Goldberg

Animals in the House

1.
Some animals never leave us:
mice between cracks
in the cinderblocks, insects the size
of pores of skin.
How can you know where they wait?
Pain unhinges doors and windows.
Starlings funnel into the openings,
amazed at the low ceiling where a katydid,
firegreen, moves slowly
into the light around the fixture.

It's no use, my husband says,
let them stay. He turns off the light
but I'm already asleep, dreaming
of an animal without a face
when he lifts my nightgown.

Don't be afraid, he whispers,
it's time. So I wake and touch him.

Then the beating above us, the cat
leaping to show how easily
a wren pins its wings around itself.

2.
When I had a migraine that lasted a week
I took off my clothes and shut
the light, the door, the shades
and had nightmares
of running, running in my bathing suit
near Coney Island at midnight
with four men after me
and I knew they had knives.

I stayed in the bedroom all week
until the evening when I could
stand and walk outside,
sit on the lawnchair
and watch the squirrels, fat flies,
bluejays diving into the house.

3.
Once I pretended to be the animal.
My best friend dead, I ran—
the sidewalk ending, the sidewalk beginning,
the streetlights coming on, my legs feeling nothing.
I ran away because this is what animals in pain do.

4.
The animals get in,
the animals take over

At synagogue an old woman stood
to say Kaddish for her dead husband.
She couldn't finish.
Hands lowered her to her seat

where she would be next Friday night
and the next—a year of saying words
she knows by heart without understanding

like a lullaby to sing the animals asleep.

5.
I'm pregnant now, an animal
with an animal inside.

I drink water all day
and dream of butter
on French bread, cakes
dipped in Amaretto.
The baby kicks or punches
but soon it will sink toward an opening

and I'm afraid of how
I'll fight the contractions
keep standing up, trying to leave
the delivery room, telling the nurses
it's too hard

until the pain makes me stop
being anything but an animal
who screams, who sing-screams,
caught in the place
where they go
to hunt in the dark,
to wait for the scent,
the wind to stop,

to throw themselves down,
throw all of themselves
down for this.

Then there is no house,
just two animals who hold each other and sleep a long time.

Epilogue

Who or what was in the past? Does it matter that Langston Hughes grew up in Lawrence or that William Stafford studied at the University in the 1950's? Does it matter that in the early 1960's Professor Ed Grier was working on Walt Whitman and Terrance Williams was at Special Collections? Probably. And it may be that David Ignatow in the late 1960's as visiting writer was heating things up with an influx of poets from the Lower East Side–Ed Sanders, Tuli Kupferberg and Jackson McLow. followed by Allen Ginsberg. Ed Dorn came and stayed writing on *Gunslinger.* ("The west begins at 701 Massachusetts street.") 701 Mass, one block from the Kaw River...the Eldridge Hotel. "Helen" publishing broadsides, Denise Levertov visiting, *Grist* publishing Carole Berge and Lee Chapman, *Cottonwood* with a poem by "Linda" Heijnian. But Kansas couldn't hold all the poets. She gave up Charlie Blymell, Bruce Conners, Dennis Hopper, Michael McClure to San Francisco. In return came John Fowler with the Abington Bookstore and *Grist* magazine (Olson, Burroughs, Hunke, Creeley, Ginsberg, et al). The Tansy from Olson's Gloucester to John Moritz in Lawrence grew to another bookstore and magazine and continues today as Tansy Press. Underground papers included *BeanNews*, City Moon and the *Vortex* of the 1960's. In the 1970's *Tellus* magazine was published and edited by Steve Bunch and combined with the continued efforts of folk like Steve Addiss, Stan Lombardo and Caryn Mirriam-Goldberg (all employed by KU) to bring their energy "down the hill" and into the community. *Cottonwood Review* off Mt. Oread through the University continues today as a respected journal and press edited over the years by James Grauerholz, Bill Knief, Denise Low, Phil and George Wedge, Lee Chapman and Ken Irving. Readings then at the University and in the beer joints and in basement coffee house, The Fiery Furnace...and today in bars, library, community art center, new age coffee houses and Poetry Slams at the local topless bar...it does continue.

For sure and for the better of us all, there is no "school" of poetics known as the Lawrence School. Thank God for that. Why? Who knows. There just isn't. There are connections enough and it is easy enough to collect these poets under one cover. Here now in your hands, from this place called Lawrence...named by her poets, described from every direction or none at all...simply the sense of being *here* and writing...what flows through to the page. What we have is a collection from this place...for you...the reader...to look through and perhaps hopefully...to join in *to* some place known as Lawrence, Kansas.

Jim McCrary

Biographies

Stephen Addiss is a composer, painter, calligraphers, and art historian. A student of John Cage, he is particularly interested in the interconnections of the arts. He has been an occasional poet for more than four decades.

Tony Allard teaches performance art and installation at the Kansas City Art Institute, where he is Visiting Artist. He has performed his work in San Francisco, Dallas, Kansas City, Chicago and at colleges and sites throughout the Midwest. His articles and reviews appear in *New Art Examiner, Journal of Dramatic Theory and Criticism, Kansas Quarterly,* and *Forum Magazine.* He has done radio performance on *From Art to Microchip,* a public radio show, and *The World Mix,* a live production for KCUR FM.

James Bogan attended the University of Kansas in the late sixties before being driven by General Hershey to the wilds of the Missouri Ozarks, where he has since taught writing, literature, art history, and film at the University of Missouri-Rolla–a Jayhawker amongst the Bushwackers.

Edward L. Brunt, born in Omaha, Nebraska, is a Lawrence police officer. His hobbies include Tae-Kwon-Do, guitar, piano, harmonica, dance, and writing poetry. His reason for writing—a reflection of personal growth.

A native Kansan, **Stephen Bunch** has lived in Lawrence off and on since 1968 and continuously from 1976. From 1978 to 1988 he was the editor and publisher of *Tellus,* a literary magazine, and *Carpool,* a chapbook of poems by Donald Levering. He also co-published, with Cottonwood Review Press, *A Kansas Sequence,* by Victor Contoski.

Victor Contoski is a former U.S. postal chess champion, but his current interest is shogi (Japanese chess). He is captain of the U.S. postal shogi team. His *Selected Poems* is scheduled to be published by New Rivers Press. He teaches creative writing and American Literature at KU.

Brian Daldorph is from Bishop's Stortford, England. He moved to the U.S. in 1983 to go to school at Illinois State. In 1990 he finished his Ph.D. at the University of Illinois. He is an Assistant Professor in the English Department of the University of Kansas, author of three poetry chapbooks, and editor of *Coal City Review.*

Roy Gridley makes a living teaching at the Unviersity of Kansas. He has published two small chapbooks of poetry (PRC Dairy--June 1982 and Pieces of China), two books on Robert Browning and articles on the Great Plains of North America.

Jane Hoskinson is an editor and writer for the University of Kansas Office of University Relations. She has published poems in *Cincinnati Poetry Review, Cottonwood, WomanSpirit, Midwifery Today* and *Confluence.* She is on the poetry staff of *Cottonwood* magazine.

Ken Irby first resided in Lawrence as an undergraduate at KU and returned to live here in 1977. His most recent book is *Call Steps* (Station Hill/Tansy, 1992)

Kathleen Johnson is a graduate student at the University of Kansas studying the interrelationship of literature and the visual arts. She has had poems published in *Riverrun, Blue Unicorn, Earthwise Poetry Review, The Midwest Quarterly,* and the *Cotton Review* anthology and *Kansas Women Writers.*

Michael Johnson is chair of the Department of English at KU. His poems and poetic translations have been published widely in journals and little magazines. His two most recent collections are *The Birds From I Know Where* (Cottonwood Press, 1989) and *Ecphrases* (Woodley Press, 1989).

Philip Kimball is a fiction writer who was the champion of the first Lawrence Poetry Grand Slam in December in 1991, and whose poem "breaking the plains" won first prize in the 1992 Kansas Voices contest. He lives in Lawrence.

Mary Klayder has lived in Lawrence, Kansas, off and on for almost twenty-five years. She is currently teaching literature at the University of Kansas.

Stanley Lombardo plays snooker at King Arthur's, sits at the Kansas Zen Center, teaches classics at KU, and translates Greek poetry at home, all in Lawrence.

Denise Low is a fifth generation Kansas who has mostly lived in Lawrence since 1967. She teaches at Haskell Indian Junior College and has recent books from Penthe Publishing Co., *Tulip Elegies: An Alchemy of Writing,* and Mulberry Press, *Vanishing Point.* She has received awards for her poetry from the Kansas Arts Commission, Roberts Foundation, Seaton-Kansas Quarterly Awards and Pushcart Press.

Jim McCrary received his MA in Creative Writing from California State University, Sonoma. In 1992 two books were published: *And/Or* from e.g. books, St. Paul, Minnesota and *West of Mass* from Tansy Books, Lawrence, Kansas. He co-curates readings at the Lawrence Art Center and the Poetry Slam at the Flamingo Club in Lawrence, Kansas. He teaches Contemporary American Poetics and workshops at the Lawrence Arts Center.

Caryn Mirriam-Goldberg writes, reads and teaches in Lawrence. A native of New Jersey (most ridiculed state), she plans to live in Kansas (second most ridiculed state) the rest of her life. Her poems have appeared in many journals, including *Nimrod, Louisville Review* and *River City Review* and have won several awards. She does frequent readings and writing workshops in the region.

John Moritz was born in Gary, Indiana, 1946, and attended various miliary schools around the Chicago area. In 1967 he moved to Lawrence and enrolled at the University of Kansas which he attended for two years. Since then he learning printing and has been publishing Tansy books ever since. Last July he married Sharon in Sitka, Alaska, under the totem, raven-stealing-moon.

Karen Ohnesorge-Fick, raised in eastern Tennessee, went to graduate school at New York University before moving to Lawrence in 1986. A teacher and painter, as well as a poet, Karen has worked for six years as director of Ottawa University's Academic Achievement Center and instructor of General Education.

Marlon Ohnesorge-Fick was born in Olathe, Kansas, and lived in Lawrence from 1978 to 1983, and again from 1986 to 1992. He received a Master's degree in poetics from New York University (1986), and a Ph.d. in English from the University of Kansas in 1992. His poetry has appeared in *Antioch Review, Mudfish, Denver Quarterly, South Coast Poetry Journal, Kansas Quarterly,* and *Taos Review.* He is married to Karen Ohnesorge-Fick and has a son, Walt.

Trish Reeves received a 1988 National Endowment for the Arts fellowship grant in creative writing. Also in 1988, she was a Yaddo Fellow and her book, *Returning the Question,* won the Cleveland State Unviersity Poetry Center Prize. Her poems have appeared in *Ploughshares, Ironwood, New Letters, Pequod, Prairie Schooner, The Ploughshares Poetry Reader,* etc. Since 1991 she has worked as an instructor at Haskell Indian Junior College.

Judith Roitman is a mathematician at the University of Kansas. Her poems have most recently appeared in *Caliban, Abraxas,* and *River City Review.*

Anne Wallace was born in Lawrence, grew up in Topeka, and lived in Lawrence for fifteen years after she came back to study at the University of Kansas. She teaches nineteenth-century British literature at the Unviersity of Southern Mississippi in Hattiesburg, Mississippi, where she lives with her daughter, Sarah.

George Wedge, Associate Professor of English at the University of Kansas, has been Editor of *Cottonwood* since 1985 and has performed editorial functions on other literary magazines and scholarly journals since the 1950s. His poems have appeared in a number of small magazines and quarterlies.

Phil Wedge is a Lecturer in English at the University of Kasnas and Poetry Editor of *Cottonwood* Magazine and Press. His poetry has recently appeared in *The American Scholar, Kansas Quarterly, Stone Country, Wind,* and *High Plains Literary Review,* among others. His work has also recently appeared in *Hummers, Knucklers, and Slow Curves* (University of Illinois Press), an anthology of baseball poetry.

Acknowledgements

Grateful acknowledgment is made for permission to reprint the following:

Bunch, Stephen
"Inland, See" was first published in *White Pine Journal* (issue 24/25), Winter 1981. It was reprinted in *Confluence*, Cottonwood Review Press, 1984.
"Dog Days" was first published in *The Vanderbilt Review* (volume I, issue 1), Spring 1980 and reprinted in *Confluence*, Cottonwood Review Press, 1984.
"The Choice" first appeared in *Tellus* (issue 11), Summer 1988.

Hoskinson, Jane
"Nova" was first published in *Cincinnati Poetry Review* (issue 15), "The Midwife's Workbook" series.

Irby, Ken
"I have fetched phoenix papers" published in *Notus* 9 (1991).
"I met the Angel Sus" published in *Call Steps* (Barrytown, NY/Lawrence, KS: Station Hill/Tansy Press, 1992).
"late in the Winter" published in *Call Steps*.
"a silence in the Central Tree" published in *Call Steps*.
[for Jonathan Williams' 50th birthday] published in *Call Steps*.
"the place of the Lord of Soil" published in *Catalpa* (Lawrence, KS: Tansy Press, 1977).
"at dawn, visitors" published in *Catalpa*.

Johnson, Kathleen
"Farm Wife" was previously published in *The Midwest Quarterly*.
"To My First Lover, An Auto Mechanic" was previously published in *Earthwise Review*.

Low, Denise
"Tulip Elegy II" first appeared in the Kansas City Star, reprinted in Tulip Elegies: *An Alchemy of Writing*, (Lawrence, KS: Penthe Publishing Co., 1992).
"Tulip Elegy VIII" was first published in *Tulip Elegies; An Alchemy of Writing*

McCrary, Jim
"Address Unknown" was first published in *Exquisite Corpse*; also included in the collection *West of Mass*, Tansy Books, Lawrence, KS, October 1992.

Mirriam-Goldberg, Caryn
"About Desire" first appeared in *The Exquisite Corpse*.
"Diana, the Huntress..." first appeared in *Chiron Review*.

Ohnesorge-Fick, Karen
"Ma's Ghost" was first published in *Ploughshares*, volume 13, #4.

Wedge, Phil
"In Retrospect" first appeared in *Stone Country*.
"Van Gogh's 'Crows Over a Cornfield'" first appeared in *Kansas Quarterly*.
"The Sandpits" first appeared in *Kansas Quarterly*.
"Car Keys" first appeared in *Amelia*.